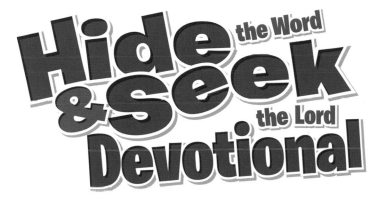

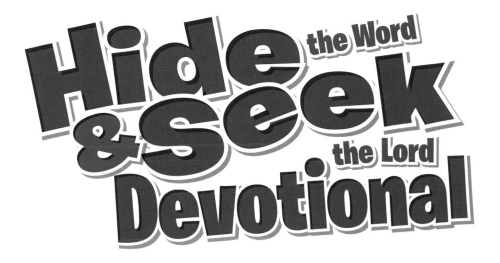

Hide the Word & Seek the Lord Devotional

Finding God's Way by Knowing God's Word!

Created by **Stephen Elkins**

Illustrated by **Amanda Gulliver**

Tommy NELSON®

A Division of Thomas Nelson Publishers

NASHVILLE   DALLAS   MEXICO CITY   RIO DE JANEIRO

Published in Nashville, Tennessee, by Tommy Nelson. Tommy Nelson is a registered trademark of Thomas Nelson, Inc.

Page design by Lori Lynch and Mandi Cofer.

Tommy Nelson® titles may be purchased in bulk for educational, business, fund-raising, or sales promotional use. For information, please e-mail SpecialMarkets@ThomasNelson.com.

Library of Congress Cataloging-in-Publication Data

Elkins, Stephen.
    Hide and seek devotional / by Stephen Elkins ; illustrated by Amanda Gulliver.
      p. cm.
    ISBN 978-1-4003-1648-9 (hardcover : alk. paper)
    1. Children—Religious life—Juvenile literature. 2. Bible stories, English. 3. Children—Prayers and devotions. I. Gulliver, Amanda. II. Title.
    BV4571.3.E45 2012
    220.9'505—dc23

2011025325

Printed in China
11 12 13 14 15 RRD 5 4 3 2 1

Mfr: RR Donnelley / Shenzhen, China / November 2011 / PPO# 123997

**For a free download of all 52 songs and
Bible stories narrated by Kirk Cameron,
visit www.thomasnelson.com/hideandseek!**

Dear Parents,

Do you remember the first thing that happens to Jesus after coming up out of the baptismal waters? Just as His ministry begins, He is led into the wilderness . . . a very uncomfortable place. There He is tempted. His ministry and his credentials as the Son of God are challenged. If He sins now, all will be lost. How does Jesus respond?

By *knowing* and *applying* God's Word! Preparedness is the answer. Christ demonstrates its importance, and He is able to stand the tempter's test. How? By *knowing* and *applying* God's Word! That's what the *Hide & Seek Devotional* is all about: knowing and applying God's Word! The same method Christ used in the wilderness, your child will use on the playground! It's easy . . . and it's all right here in this very special book!

Jesus said: "It is written," then He quoted the appropriate verse that applied to the challenge before him. *Hide & Seek* will teach children to know and apply Scripture to their own challenges by using Scripture songs, devotions, prayer, and the familiar device of A to Z organization. What a powerful defense!

So, what's the *A* verse? The *B* verse? The *C* verse?

A—How **Awesome** is the LORD . . .
B—On my **Bed** I remember you . . .
C—God **Created** the heavens and the earth . . .
D—My mouth will **Declare** your praise . . .

To **know** and **apply** the Word . . . that's *Hide & Seek*.

To develop a stronger **relationship** with the Father . . . that's *Hide & Seek*.

To have **fun** learning the most important lessons in life . . . that's *Hide & Seek*.

The net result is **obedience**: for we as parents and educators will accomplish what is commanded of us. We will train up our children in the Way—not *a* way—*the* Way they should go. And our children will not depart from it.

Our mutual **prayer**: When our children face temptation, they will be prepared. They will *know* and *apply* God's Word.

Your child can find God's Way by knowing God's Word— it's all right here.

Hide-and-seek . . . *you're it!*

Stephen Elkins

CONTENTS

Old Testament

CONTENTS
New Testament

How **Awesome** is the Lord Most High.

Psalm 47:2

Moses Parts the Red Sea (around 1446 BC)

Once, Moses and the people of Israel had a really awesome day. They were about to be attacked by the Egyptian army. With the desert in front of them and the Red Sea behind them, there was no way of escape. But God is an awesome God. He parted the Red Sea, and God's people walked to safety! What an awesome day!

You can read the whole story in your Bible in the book of Exodus, chapter 14!

How Awesome Is the Lord

How awesome, how awesome is the Lord our God!
He is good.
How awesome, how awesome is our God!
He is an awesome God!

Devotion: Greater Than Great

Lots of days are very good. A day full of sunny, blue skies is a very good day. Other days can be great. A day at the beach, flying kites with your friends is a great day. But every now and then, you have a really awesome day. An awesome day is better than good. It's even greater than great. It's the very best day of all!

God is more than good. God is greater than great. God is awesome! The Bible says there is none like Him. He is awesome because He can do all things. There is no problem too big for God. He can solve any problem, even if He has to part a sea! Got a little problem? Got a giant problem? Remember, God is better than good and greater than great. God is an awesome God!

♟ HIDE THE WORD

How awesome is the LORD Most High. —Psalm 47:2

👁 SEEK THE LORD

Three Awesome Things

God has proven time and again that He's an awesome God. His mighty deeds bear witness! They bring us a sense of "awe," which is great wonder and respect. Moses said in Exodus 8:10, "There is no one like the LORD our God." Can you think of three "awe"-some things our God has done? (Hint: He created something in the sky, He created things that live in the ocean, and He sent somebody to save us!)

✝ PRAY TO GOD

Dear God, You are indeed *awesome*. There is truly no one like You. You stand alone as the Creator of all things. The heavens declare Your glory. The stars show Your handiwork. Thank You, Lord, for all You alone have done. How *awesome* You are! Amen.

Answers: The sun, moon, and stars; whales, sharks, and dolphins; Jesus

On my Bed I remember you; I think of you through the watches of the night.

Psalm 63:6

David Loved to Pray (around 1025 BC)

David the shepherd boy loved to pray too! He spent many nights alone on the Judean hillside watching his sheep. He watched as the moon moved across the night sky. He heard the sounds of wild animals in the distance. So on his bed, before he went to sleep, David would remember his Lord and all His promises. He could sleep soundly knowing that God had heard his prayers and was watching from above.

You can read more about David the shepherd boy in the book of 1 Samuel, chapters 16 and 17!

On My Bed I Will Remember You

On my bed, I remember You.
On my bed, I remember You, Lord.
On my bed, I remember You.
I think of You through the watches of the night.
I think of You through the watches of the night.

Devotion: Whisper a Little Prayer

After a busy day at school or play, it's nice to get into your bed at night. It's a very special time. You might fix your pillow just right and get snuggled up in the covers. When the lights go out, your eyes start getting heavy. You think about all the things you're going to do tomorrow. It's a perfect time to whisper a little prayer. Tonight, as you lie down on your bed, remember God's wonderful promises. He promises to love you. He promises to guide you. He promises to watch over you all through the night. Soon, instead of counting sheep, you'll find yourself counting your blessings.

🔑 HIDE THE WORD

On my bed I remember you; I think of you through the watches of the night. —Psalm 63:6

👁 SEEK THE LORD

Keep Your Promises

When we make a promise, we give our word that we will do something, no matter what happens. It's a pledge that should never be broken.

Have you ever made a promise? Pour yourself a small glass of milk. Now, if you're sure you can, promise your mom you will drink it all. If you promised, drink it all, no matter what. Did you keep your promise? Question: Should you make a promise to drink the whole gallon of milk? No. You should only make promises you can keep. Remember, God keeps every promise, no matter how hard it is!

✝ PRAY TO GOD

Dear Father, the Bible is full of Your promises. And it is so good to know that You will keep every one of them, no matter what! You promise to help me (Hebrews 13:6). You promise to answer my prayers (Jeremiah 33:3). Best of all, You promise to save me (Romans 10:13). Thank You, Lord, for all Your unfailing promises! Amen.

God **Created** the heavens and the earth.

Genesis 1:1

The Creation Story (Day 1)

God made the heavens and the earth with only His words. He spoke, and the heavens came to be. He spoke again, and the earth was made. He used no paper or string, no wood or nails. In fact, He used nothing at all. He is so powerful and creative that He made everything with only His words!

You can read this story in the book of Genesis, chapters 1 and 2!

God Created the Heavens

In the beginning! Oh, in the beginning!
In the beginning,
God created the heavens and the earth.
In the beginning,
God created the heavens and the earth,
The heavens and the earth.

Devotion: God Is Our Creator

It's really fun to make things with your own hands. With a little glue and an hour or two, you can make almost anything. You and Mom can make a kite out of paper and string. You can help Dad make a birdhouse out of wood and nails. But do you know what God made?

The Bible says that God created the heavens and the earth. It also says God created you. It says that He knew you before you were even born. And all that God creates is good. Thank You, God, for this wonderful world You have created.

⚷ HIDE THE WORD

God created the heavens and the earth. —Genesis 1:1

👁 SEEK THE LORD

Things God Made

The Bible tells us that in the beginning God created all things. He filled an empty universe with stars, planets, and every living creature. How did He do it? Not with a hammer and nails! The Bible says our mighty God simply spoke and, with His word, all things came to be! Can you draw a picture of three things God created in the beginning? (Hint: Some of them were on Noah's ark.)

✝ PRAY TO GOD

Dear God, truly there is none like You. Who could do the things You've done? You alone created the heavens and the earth. You alone had the power to make mountaintops stretch up into the sky. You alone filled the sea with fish and whales. For this and so much more, we give You praise. Your deeds are mighty; Your power so great! Amen.

My mouth will Declare your praise.

Psalm 51:15

Solomon Was a Wise Man (reigned from 970 to 930 BC)

Solomon was the wisest man ever to live. He knew a lot of words. He used his words to write over one thousand songs to the Lord. He also wrote three thousand proverbs. What a difference his words made! He used them to declare the praise of the Lord, just like his father David. It was Solomon who wrote: "Saying the right word at the right time is so pleasing!" (Proverbs 15:23 ICB). His mouth and his words declared God's praise!

You can read the wise words of Solomon in the book of Proverbs!

My Mouth Will Declare Your Praise

My mouth will declare Your praises, O Lord!
My mouth will declare Your praises, O Lord!
I praise You for the moon at night,
Praise You for the stars,
Praise You, Lord, for all You've done,
Praise You for who You are!

Devotion: Believing Out Loud

So many different kinds of words can come out of your mouth. You can speak a word of kindness. You can say "thank you." You can use words to comfort someone in need. You can even shout an alarm: "Help!" Your words can really make a difference in the lives of others.

How will people know that your God is a wonderful God unless you tell them? You have to show them with your actions and tell them the story of God. Sure, you believe in the Lord on the inside. But you have to start believing out loud. You can make every day a show-and-tell day. Show and tell them about God's love!

⚷ HIDE THE WORD

My mouth will declare your praise. —Psalm 51:15

👁 SEEK THE LORD

Love Letter

There are seven billion people living in this world. And many of them have not heard about the love of God. Some of them may live on your street. They may sit beside you at school. Can you think of someone who needs to know about Jesus? Write a short letter to that person and tell them Jesus loves them. Ask God to give you just the right words to "declare" His praise.

✝ PRAY TO GOD

Dear Lord, Solomon was very wise. He knew lots of words. But I only know a few. Help me to use the words I know to tell others about Jesus. Give me the courage to declare Your praise. Then open their eyes so that they might see Jesus! Amen.

Let **Everything** that has breat~~h~~ ...se the Lord.

Psalm 150:6

...che Flood (around 2344 BC)

Noah ...hed in the funny smell of thousands of ... packed into one boat. But he spoke out word ... praise to God, because he loved the Lord! God told Noah to build an ark and gather all the animals together, two of every kind. Noah obeyed. The flood waters came and destroyed all the evil people. But Noah and his family were saved!

You can read the whole story in Genesis, chapters 6 to 9!

Let Everything That Has Breath Praise the Lord

Let everything, everything that has breath,
Let everything, everything that has breath,
Praise the Lord, praise the Lord, I say!
Can you hear me today?
Come on, every girl and boy,
Make a mighty noise and praise the Lord!

Devotion: Share the Gift

You have breath, right? What do you use it for? Dogs can use their breath to bark. Cats can use their breath to meow. Birds can sing, and lions can roar. But only people can use their breath to speak. You can use words to express your thoughts. But most of all, you should use your breath to praise the Lord!

If you have breath, you are alive. And if you are alive, you should give thanks to the Lord for all He has done. You should praise Him, for life is the most important gift God has given to you. Share the gift. Tell others about God's love. And as long as you have breath, praise the Lord.

⚷ HIDE THE WORD

Let everything that has breath praise the LORD.
—Psalm 150:6

👁 SEEK THE LORD

A Thank-You Note

Why is it that boys and girls all over the world praise the Lord? Because they come to know how much God loves them! They want to say, "Thank You, Lord, for loving me!" They praise Him for answering their prayers and helping them through times of trouble. It's good to praise the Lord for all He has done. Can you think of something you are thankful for? Draw a picture of it and write, "Thank You, Lord!" under your picture. Place it on your refrigerator as your praise reminder.

✝ PRAY TO GOD

Dear Lord, I praise You right now. I praise You for who You are and all the mighty deeds You have done. I know You are an awesome God. I know You keep Your promises, and You are the maker of all things. For that, and so much more, let everything that has breath give You praise! Amen.

A **Friend** loves at all times.

Proverbs 17:17

Jonathan and David Were Friends (around 1010 BC)

Jonathan and David were best friends. Jonathan's father was the king of Israel, so David and Jonathan stayed in the palace. They enjoyed being together. They respected each other. Jonathan gave David his robe and tunic, even his sword and his bow! When bad times came, Jonathan showed David that he was a true friend.

You can read the whole story in 1 Samuel, chapters 18 to 20!

A Friend Loves at All Times

Oh, a friend loves at all times!
Oh, a friend loves at all times!
Morning, noon, or night,
A friend is a delight,
For a friend loves at all times!

Devotion: A Friend You Can Count On

There's nothing better than having a good friend you can count on—someone who's always there in good times and bad. Someone you can talk to and someone who'll listen. That's the kind of friend you should try to be to others. "Fair-weather" friends seem to disappear when things get tough. But a real friend is always there to give a smile, to listen, and to help!

Real friendship is based on love and a giving spirit. Jonathan had a giving spirit. You, too, can show your friendship by being giving of your time, your abilities, and even sharing your things to help others. A friend loves at all times—the good times, the bad times . . . anytime. That's what true friendship is all about!

⚷ HIDE THE WORD

A friend loves at all times. —Proverbs 17:17

◉ SEEK THE LORD

Tick-Tock, the Friendship Clock

The Bible says that a friend loves at *all* times, not just some of the time. So let's make a Friendship Clock to help us remember what the Bible says. Using a paper plate, draw the round face of a clock. You can put the numbers one through twelve around the edge of the plate. Now, in the middle of the clock, write our Bible verse, "A friend loves at all times." Your Friendship Clock will be a happy reminder to love your friends at *all* times.

✝ PRAY TO GOD

Dear God, the Bible teaches us that You love at all times. It tells me that You are always patient and kind. You even loved us when we didn't love You. Thank You, Father, for loving me like that. Help me to love my friends that very same way. I want to be more like You every day! Amen.

A **Gentle** answer turns away wrath.

Proverbs 15:1

Jesus Gave a Gentle Answer (around AD 29)

The religious leaders and teachers brought a woman to Jesus. She had broken the law. These leaders had angry hearts. They thought she should be killed with stones. They asked Jesus if He thought they were doing the right thing. But Jesus answered, "If any one of you is without sin, let him be the first to throw a stone" (John 8:7). Suddenly, it got very quiet. They all walked away, ashamed. Jesus' soft answer turned them away and saved the young woman.

You can read this story in John, chapter 8!

A Gentle Answer

A gentle answer turns away the wrath
Of those who come your way.
I say, a gentle answer calms the voice,
Stills the heart; it's heaven's choice.

Devotion: Speak a Gentle Word

People can have different views on the same subject. Some like the rain; some do not. Some like cold; some like it hot. Sometimes differences can cause tempers to flare. If you're not careful, your disagreement can turn into an argument. In those times, you should be very careful with your words. It is more difficult to settle a disagreement when someone is angry.

Sometimes, you may have disagreements with others. Even friends and family may get very angry. If this happens, it is always best to do what Jesus did. He spoke a gentle answer. Shouting unkind words at each other won't help you settle your argument. Be like Jesus. Speak a gentle word.

🔑 HIDE THE WORD

A gentle answer turns away wrath.
—Proverbs 15:1

👁 SEEK THE LORD

A Gentle Warrior

Gentleness is a fruit of the Spirit (Galatians 5:22–23). We are able to speak in gentle tones because God gives us the strength! Without Him, we could never be gentle. If our words are gentle, we help calm those who may be angry.

It takes courage to speak gently. Let's try it! Pretend someone has just said an unkind thing to you. Instead of returning unkind words back to them, practice this gentle answer in a gentle voice: "I'm sorry if I have upset you." Good job! Now you're becoming a "gentle warrior"!

✝ PRAY TO GOD

Dear Lord, gentleness is not a very popular idea today. Some think being gentle is weak. But, Lord, You have taught me to be a "gentle warrior," to fight anger with kindness. I know that the most hurtful wars begin with hateful words, so fill my heart with Your Spirit of gentleness. Let peace in this world begin with my words. Amen.

H

Love the LORD your God with all your **Heart** and with all your soul and with all your strength.

Deuteronomy 6:5

The Rich Young Ruler (around AD 30)

A rich young man once came to Jesus. He asked what he must do to have eternal life. Jesus said that he must keep all the commandments. The young man said that he had kept all the commandments. Then Jesus said that he should sell all he owned and give to the poor. But the young man could not do this because he loved the things he owned more than he loved the Lord. He didn't love God with all of his heart.

You can read this story in Mark, chapter 10!

Love the Lord Your God

God wants us to really love Him,
Love Him with all our hearts,
Night or day, work or play.
If you travel far away,
It doesn't matter wherever you are.
You know that God wants us to really love Him.

Devotion: Love with a Whole Heart

Twenty anxious girls sat down on the gym floor. Coach Maxwell came into the room and spoke. "If you are going to play basketball for the Thunder Cats, I will be here every evening, Monday through Friday, from 4:00 to 7:00. You will need to be here every day for practice."

Emily's hand slowly went up into the air. "I have piano lessons on Tuesdays at 5:00. May I be excused for that?"

The coach answered, "Absolutely not!" Emily loved playing the piano more than she loved basketball. She would not be able to try out for basketball. She could not give her all to the team.

Just like Coach Maxwell wanted the Thunder Cats to give their all if they joined the basketball team, God wants you to love Him with your whole heart. If you are half-hearted in your love for Him, you may be saving the other half for the things of this world. Nothing in this world should keep you from heaven. Today, love God with all your heart and see the difference!

♀ HIDE THE WORD

Love the LORD your God with all your heart and with all your soul and with all your strength. —Deuteronomy 6:5

👁 SEEK THE LORD

A Few Favorite Things

Make a list of your five favorite things. It might include your bike or an electronic game of some kind. Now, list them from most favorite to least favorite. Let's pretend that Jesus is coming to visit you this weekend. Like the rich young man we read about, He may ask you to give up some things. Which of the things on your list could you give up if Jesus asked? Remember, nothing we own should be more important than serving God. Learn to love God with all your heart!

✝ PRAY TO GOD

Dear Lord, I know that I must love You more than the things in this world. The rich young ruler couldn't do it, but I want to! I am learning to love You with all of my heart. But I still have a long way to go. Lord, help me to love You with *all* of my heart, for that is what You have asked of me. Amen.

So God created man in his own **Image.**

Genesis 1:27

Adam and Eve (Day 6)

God made human beings in His own image. Adam and Eve were perfect in every way. God put them in the Garden of Eden where they would have everything they needed. God blessed them and said, "Have many children and grow in number. Fill the earth and be its master. . . . Rule over every living thing that moves on the earth" (Genesis 1:28 ICB). And then God said it is very good!

You can read the whole story in Genesis, chapter 1!

God Created Man in His Own Image

God created, so God created,
God created, so God created,
God created man in His own image, oh, yeah!
We know God made a woman.
We know God made a man.
We know He created them in His image.
Please understand.

Devotion: House of Mirrors

Do you remember a time when the circus came to town? Did you go into the house of mirrors? You probably couldn't believe how funny it made you look! In one mirror, you looked short and fat. In another, you appeared to be tall and skinny. Your image would change with every mirror. It would be easy to forget what you really looked like!

Some people have forgotten what they are supposed to look like on the inside. They were created in the image of God. Yet, because of their sinful habits, it's hard to see God in them. God is joyful and loving. You should be too! God is honest and trustworthy. You should be too! God is faithful and just. And yes—you should be too! This world can bend your image like a house of mirrors. But don't forget, you were made in the image of God!

♟ HIDE THE WORD

So God created man in his own image.
—Genesis 1:27

👁 SEEK THE LORD

Frog to Prince

There is an old fairytale about a frog who turned into a man. In fact, he became a handsome young prince. How did it happen? Believe it or not, with a magic kiss! How silly! But some people today tell us that frogs did, indeed, turn into a man. Not by a magic kiss, but by the "magic" of time. It's called "evolution." Neither a short kiss nor a long time can create a man. Only God can make a prince. And only God can make a frog (Genesis 1:24). Can you think of something God made that frogs like? (Hint: Where they swim, what they eat, and what they sit on!)

✝ PRAY TO GOD

God, I know You made me. I was created in Your image. I am not an accident of "time plus slime," but rather, Your marvelous creation! But I wonder if someone had a special pair of glasses to see inside my heart, would they see the image of You or something else? Lord, keep me from sin and help me to be everything You created me to be. Amen.

Answers: Ponds, flies, and lily pads

The Joy of the Lord is your strength.

Nehemiah 8:10

Paul Lives a Godly Life (around AD 59-61)

Paul knew how difficult it was to work toward a great reward. When he chose to live a godly life, people made fun of him, and he was even put in jail! But Paul kept going, knowing that the reward in the end would be worth it all. And at the end of his struggles, he looked back and said, "I have fought the good fight, I have finished the race, I have kept the faith. Now there is in store for me the crown of righteousness, which the Lord . . . will award to me on that day" (2 Timothy 4:7–8).

You can read the whole story in 2 Timothy!

The Joy of the Lord

I've got the joy, joy, joy down in my heart!
I've got the joy, joy, joy down in my heart,
'Cause the joy of the Lord is my strength!
Yes, indeed!
The joy of the Lord is my strength!

Devotion: The Reward to Come

Robert was a member of the Cub Scouts. There was nothing he wanted more than to earn his Arrow of Light award! So when other kids were playing video games or watching cartoons, Robert worked hard to reach his goal. He knew the sacrifice would be worth it when they presented the badge to him at the Pack meeting. The thought of the joy of that moment kept him going!

When you have a tough job to do, just thinking about the reward to come is enough to keep you going! In your Christian journey, you may face many trials. But the joy of knowing that God's servants are bound for heaven will help you through the day, the year, even the rest of your life. Yes, the joy of the Lord is your strength to reach the finish line!

🔑 HIDE THE WORD

The joy of the Lord is your strength. —Nehemiah 8:10

👁 SEEK THE LORD

Don't Quit!

Have you ever thought about quitting? When the job got too hard, were you tempted to walk away? Everyone has moments like that; especially when you are working for the Lord. But don't quit! The Lord promises us a great reward if we finish the work He gives us. It's like doing homework. It's much easier to get the job done if you imagine yourself looking at an A on your report card. The A becomes your strength, your reason to finish the job. Let the joy of the Lord be your strength, your reason to finish His work!

✝ PRAY TO GOD

Dear Lord, to think that one day I will stand before You face to face . . . what a joyful day that will be! I want You to be proud of me on that day. So I have fixed in my mind the joy of that moment. And that joy becomes my strength, my reason to finish the work You have given me. When I fall down, when I feel like quitting, You will be my strength to get up again! Your joy is my reason to finish! Amen.

Keep my commands and you will live.

Proverbs 4:4

Jeremiah Reminds Israel (around 587 BC)

The prophet Jeremiah warned Israel to never ignore God's warnings. The nation of Israel had served and obeyed God for many years. But as time passed, the people forgot about God's commands. They began to sin more and more. Soon, an enemy of Israel came and made them their slaves. Jeremiah wept for the nation of Israel. But he reminded them that even though they had forgotten God, God had not forgotten them.

You can read this in Lamentations, chapter 3!

Keep My Commands and Live

Keep My commandments and you will live.
Keep My commandments and you will live.
If you keep My commandments,
You will live.
If you keep My commandments,
You will live; you will live.

Devotion: God's Commandments

The rain was pouring down. The wipers could barely clear the windshield. Thunder crashed and lightning filled the sky. It was only a few more miles to the bridge. Suddenly, Juan saw a very bright light up ahead. A policeman with a flare was standing in the downpour. "The bridge is out!" he shouted. "Go back!" Juan's dad thanked the policeman. His warning had saved their lives.

God's commandments show you the way and serve as a warning. They are like a light in a very dark world. They show you the right way to live your life. They are also a warning, telling you, "There's danger ahead! Don't go that way!" Every day you must choose to obey or ignore God's commands. If you obey His commands, you will live an exciting life!

🔑 HIDE THE WORD

Keep my commands and you will live. —Proverbs 4:4

👁 SEEK THE LORD

The 10 "Real Love" Commandments

Have you ever wondered what "real love" looks like? The Bible tells us. God gave Moses ten "real love" commandments. He did this so the world would know what real love looks like. People who have real love in their hearts don't steal from each other (Exodus 20:15). People who have real love in their hearts don't kill each other (Exodus 20:13). People who have real love in their hearts don't make up bad stories about each other (Exodus 20:16).

Since we know that God is love, it should be no surprise that His commandments are full of love too! Let's draw two tablets on a piece of paper. On the tablets, list the Ten Commandments. Now that's *real* love! (Hint: Look at Exodus 20.)

✝ PRAY TO GOD

Dear Lord, Your commandments show me what real love looks like. It looks like Jesus! With His love in my heart, I am able to love the way You intended. Thank You for showing me how to respect You and love others. I know that keeping Your commandments brings life. May I always show the world the *real love* of Jesus! Amen.

Your word is a **Lamp** to my feet and a light for my path.

Psalm 119:105

Paul on the Damascus Road (around AD 35)

The missionary Paul wasn't always a believer in Jesus Christ. In fact, before he became a Christian, his name was Saul. Saul spent his days looking for Christians so he could put them into prison. One day, as he neared Damascus, a bright light flashed around him. Then he heard a voice saying, "Why do you persecute me?" (Acts 9:4). Saul was afraid and asked, "Who are you?" The voice answered, "I am Jesus" (Acts 9:5). Saul was blinded by the bright light. But three days later, he could see once again. When Saul became a Christian, his name was changed to Paul. He taught many people about Jesus.

You can read the whole story in Acts, chapter 9!

Your Word Is a Lamp

Your Word is a lamp to my feet
And a light for my path.
Wherever I am going,
Your Word is a lamp to my feet
And a light for my path.

Devotion: God's Light

One summer, Lindsay visited her grandfather's farm. After dinner each night, she and Granddad would walk down a small path to the barn to check on the horses. Since the path had no lights, Granddad would carry a lantern to light the way. Granddad knew the way well, so Lindsay would stay close to him and walk in the light.

God's Word is like a lamp. It allows you to see clearly the things ahead. Without a lamp, you might stumble and fall. You may wonder what tomorrow might bring. But don't worry: God has that under control. Just stay close to your Father by praying, obeying, and studying the Bible. Walk in God's light.

⚷ HIDE THE WORD

Your word is a lamp to my feet and a light for my path.
—Psalm 119:105

👁 SEEK THE LORD

Step into the Light

What does it mean to walk in the light of God's Word? Ask your mom or dad to use a flashlight to shine a light onto the floor. (Hint: This works best in a room that's dark.) Now, step into the light. Have your mom move the light across the floor. The flashlight has become a "lamp" to your feet! As you step into its light, you are safe because you are "walking in the light." Without that light, you might bump into something, or fall and get hurt.

God's Word is like a flashlight. As long as we walk in His light, we'll be safely on the right path.

✝ PRAY TO GOD

Dear Lord, Your Word is a lamp to my feet. It shows me the way to go. It shows me what is good and what is not so good. Thank You for Your Word, which lights my way. And thank You for Jesus, who is truly the Light of the World! Amen.

"For My thoughts are not your thoughts, neither are your ways my ways," declares the Lord.

Isaiah 55:8

Joshua and the Battle of Jericho (around 1400 BC)

Joshua's army crossed the Jordan River into the Promised Land. There, they would battle the Canaanites at Jericho. But the Lord told Joshua to do a very strange thing. To win the battle, the Lord told him to march around the walls of Jericho once a day for six days. Then, on the seventh day, march again, sound the trumpets, and shout! Even though it sounded strange, Joshua obeyed the Lord. The walls of Jericho fell exactly like the Lord said they would!

You can read the whole story in Joshua, chapter 6!

My Thoughts Are Not Your Thoughts

"For My thoughts are not your thoughts,
Neither are your ways My ways,"
Declares the Lord to all who will believe.

Devotion: He Knows the Best Way

"Hiccup!" *What do I have to do to make these things go away?* Michael wondered. He walked over to Dad, opened his mouth to speak, and—"Hiccup!"

With a grin, Dad instructed, "Hold your breath and swallow ten times." Michael gave him a funny look, but unable to question him—"Hiccup!"—Michael tried it. And what do you know? The hiccups went away!

Some things just don't make sense—like the battle of Jericho. What a strange way to win a battle! Joshua's army didn't use their strength. They didn't use their weapons. They didn't need to. They simply obeyed God's command. God's ways are not your ways. Sometimes He does things a little differently than you might do them. But no matter what today may bring, you must be of good courage like Joshua. And you must trust your heavenly Father. He always knows the best way!

⚷ HIDE THE WORD

"For my thoughts are not your thoughts, neither are your ways my ways," declares the Lord. —Isaiah 55:8

👁 SEEK THE LORD

God's Way

God's way of doing things can be a bit different. I mean, who starts a prayer meeting in the belly of a fish (Jonah 2)? God would! Who would bring down a 25-foot-high stone wall with a shout (Joshua 6)? God would! Who would lay the King of kings in a manger inside a stinky cattle stall (Luke 2)? God would! God would because He wants us to know who is in control of every situation. Jonah and Joshua weren't. God was! God wants our trust to be in Him and not ourselves. Can you think of some other things God has done in a different way?

✝ PRAY TO GOD

Dear Lord, Your wisdom is beyond mine. Your power exceeds all that will ever be. You alone are Lord of all and in control of all. Work out Your plan in my life *Your* way. And when I do not understand, teach me to trust that Your way is perfect. Amen.

Answers: God created a universe with His words (Hebrews 11:3), healed blind eyes with mud (John 9), brought down a giant with a stone (1 Samuel 17), and fed 5,000 (Matthew 14) with only five loaves and two fish.

The **Name** of the LORD is a strong tower; the righteous run to it and are safe.

Proverbs 18:10

Esther Saved Her People (around 480 BC)

Esther knew there was great power in the name of the Lord. She knew it could demand authority even with kings! Esther, a Jew, was the queen of Persia. She discovered an evil plot by a man named Haman. He was planning to kill all of the Jews. Esther spoke to her cousin, Mordecai. Mordecai called upon the name of the Lord and asked Him to help His people. Esther then asked King Xerxes to help her. Her request was granted. The name of the Lord is mighty. The Lord will help His people when they call upon Him.

You can read the whole story in the book of Esther!

The Name of the Lord Is a Strong Tower

The name of the Lord is a strong tower;
The righteous run to it and are safe.

Devotion: The Name of the Lord

Smoke poured from the windows of the grocery store. A crowd soon gathered, making it difficult to pass through the street. Shoppers, reporters, and concerned onlookers all pushed against one another to watch the scene unfold. Suddenly, the crowd parted to allow one man to walk through. He didn't say a word. He didn't have to. "Fire Department" was printed across his badge, and the crowd knew he was there to help.

The name of the Lord gives you a great privilege. His name can move crowds. It can move kings. His name has great authority when you call upon God. Situations can sometimes be very frightening, and you can be tempted to give in to pressure. But don't let the situation change your faith. Let your faith change the situation. Because the name of the Lord is like a strong tower, you'll be safe with Him!

⚲ HIDE THE WORD

The name of the LORD is a strong tower;
the righteous run to it and are safe.
—Proverbs 18:10

👁 SEEK THE LORD

My God Is Bigger!

There is nothing stronger, nothing more powerful, nothing that will keep you safer than calling on the name of the Lord. God brings our biggest fears down to size when we call on Him in prayer. It's like walking into a strong tower. With the Lord, we find safety. Make a list of things you are most afraid of. Now, underneath each one write, "My God is bigger!"

✝ PRAY TO GOD

Dear Lord, the Bible says that Your name is a strong tower; the only name that saves. It says Your name is to be praised. So thank You, Father, for all You have done. Let my life be a living testimony that Your name truly is, indeed, a strong tower! Amen.

To **Obey** is better than sacrifice.

1 Samuel 15:22

King Saul Disobeyed God (around 1015 BC)

King Saul was not a UFO believer. He disobeyed the Lord. The Lord told Saul to destroy an evil enemy. Instead, Saul spared the evil king and took all the king's treasures for himself. Samuel asked Saul why he had disobeyed. Saul said that he had obeyed *most* of what God told him, and he would give God a portion of the treasures. Samuel said, "To obey is better than sacrifice" (1 Samuel 15:22). Saul was sorry for disobeying God.

You can read the whole story in 1 Samuel, chapter 15!

To Obey Is Better Than Sacrifice

To obey is better than sacrifice,
So obey the Lord, dear children.
"O"–It's the Only way to go.
"B"–Be certain it's true.
"E"–Everybody should obey.
"Y"–You and I should too.

Devotion: Obey Cheerfully

There are probably a lot of UFO Christians around your church. A missionary once spoke about UFOs.

She encouraged everyone to have **U**nwavering **F**aith and **O**bedience. Wouldn't it be awesome if every church was filled with UFOs? (But, watch out. People might think you're a little weird if you say you've seen a UFO!)

More than your time, more than your money, God wants your obedience. That is most important to Him. It is not enough to obey only a part of what He asks. But if you strive to obey Him completely, you will make God happy. God's commands are wise. Obey cheerfully.

⚑ HIDE THE WORD

To obey is better than sacrifice. —1 Samuel 15:22

👁 SEEK THE LORD

Which Way Pleases God?

Your church is raising money for a mission trip, and you want to help. On your way home from church, you find a wallet on the sidewalk with $50 inside. Wow! Should you keep the money? You could give $25 of it to the church for the mission trip! But what about the eighth commandment? The Bible says that we should not steal. What should you do? Do what the Bible says. It's better to *obey* than to sacrifice!

✝ PRAY TO GOD

God, I am learning to do the things you ask in your Word. Be patient with me, O God. I want to be a UFO believer too! Teach me to have **U**nwavering **F**aith & **O**bedience, for my obedience is better than any sacrifice. Amen.

"For I know the **Plans** I have for you," declares the LORD.

Jeremiah 29:11

Jeremiah Gives Hope (around 627 BC)

Jeremiah once sent a very special letter to the priests and prophets of Israel who were in captivity. It was a letter from God. The Jews thought that God had forgotten about them. But Jeremiah's letter from God promised that He had not forgotten them; He had great plans for them, and He would soon set them free. Hearing God's plan brought hope to the people.

You can read this in Jeremiah, chapter 29!

I Know the Plans I Have for You

"I know the plans I have for you,"
Declares the Lord.
"I know the plans I have for you,"
Declares the Lord.
"I will prosper you in all you do.
"I will be there to guide you.
"I will be a friend until the end.
"You can depend on Me."

Devotion: Surprise!

It was Maria's birthday, and no one remembered. *No cake, no candles, no party . . . how could they forget?* she wondered. Mom walked in and said, "I don't feel like cooking tonight. Let's just go to Pizza Palace to eat." When they arrived, Dad told Maria, "Go sit at that table while I order." Maria sat down and found a letter on the table with her name on it. The note inside read, "Go to the Play Room." When Maria walked into the Play Room, "Surprise!" shouted all her friends. "We've been planning this day for weeks!" Mom told her. "Did you really think we had forgotten your birthday?"

Sometimes when you're most discouraged, God is planning something wonderful for you. God knows the needs in your life, and He never forgets a single prayer. At just the time you need it most—*surprise!*—God steps in with many surprises. He has great plans for your life!

♀ HIDE THE WORD

"For I know the plans I have for you," declares the Lord. —Jeremiah 29:11

☉ SEEK THE LORD

Send Some Hope

Jeremiah's letter brought hope to God's people. They were discouraged. They thought God had forgotten them. Maybe there is someone you know who is discouraged. Maybe they are sick or have suffered a great tragedy or disappointment. You can help! Make them a card that says, "God loves you." Decorate it with stickers or color a picture. Like Jeremiah's letter, it will be a special message of hope!

✝ PRAY TO GOD

Dear Lord, I am so thankful that You have a plan for my life. I am so happy to know that You never forget about me. Knowing that I have a special place in Your heart makes me smile. Thank You for caring so much and for allowing me to be a part of Your plan. Amen.

He will **Quiet** you with his love.

Zephaniah 3:17

Jesus Calms the Storm (around AD 28)

One day, the disciples needed to calm down. As they were sailing across a lake, Jesus went to sleep in the back of the boat. And as he slept, a terrible storm came upon them. The waves were so high, the disciples were afraid. They woke Jesus and shouted, "Teacher, don't you care if we drown?" (Mark 4:38). Jesus awoke. Seeing they were afraid, He said to the sea, "Quiet! Be still!" (Mark 4:39). And the storm stopped! It was amazing! Even the wind and waves obeyed Jesus!

You can read this story in Mark 4:35–41!

He Will Quiet You with His Love

He will quiet you!
He will quiet you!
He will quiet you with His love, His love, oh!
He will quiet you!
He will quiet you!
He will quiet you with His love, His love!
Oh, God!

Devotion: Peace for a Troubled Heart

No one thought that little baby would ever stop crying! She started with a whimper that turned into a whine that grew into a cry that exploded into a *wail!* Everyone in the restaurant turned to look. Her dad bounced and patted her, but it did not help. What did the baby need? A frantic mother came running. The mom took her baby in her arms and gave her a long-awaited bottle. That was all the baby needed. She was really quiet after that!

Sometimes there is a storm brewing inside of you. Something is wrong. Maybe you have a hard decision to make. Maybe your feelings have been hurt. Maybe you've done something bad. But God can bring peace to a troubled heart. Jesus can turn all your hurts into hopes. If He can calm a wild sea, He can surely calm you! Today, ask Jesus to calm the storms in your life.

HIDE THE WORD

He will quiet you with his love. —Zephaniah 3:17

👁 SEEK THE LORD

Trust Jesus!

Have you ever been really afraid or upset? Perhaps you were frightened by a thunderstorm. The disciples were! Maybe your family was changing in some way. How do we calm down when we're really upset? In a word, TRUST. Trust the One who calmed the sea. Trust the One who calmed the brokenhearted. Trust the One who calmed the weary traveler. Trust Jesus.

Try this simple exercise. Sit quietly without saying a word for one minute. Watch the clock . . . shhh! As you wait, think to yourself, "Lord, quiet me." Remember, whether good days or bad, trust Jesus. He will quiet you with His love.

✝ PRAY TO GOD

Dear Lord, when I am afraid or really upset like the disciples were, quiet me. When I am afraid of things that are happening around me, quiet me. Teach me to trust that You are with me and will never forsake me. You know what's best for me. Quiet me with Your peace. Amen.

Remember your Creator in the days of your youth.
Ecclesiastes 12:1

Josiah, the Young King (around 622 BC)

Josiah's father was the king of Israel. But he had forgotten something very important. He had forgotten about the Lord and worshiped idols instead. Josiah became king when he was only eight years old. He destroyed the idols and sent workers to repair the temple of the Lord. Then the Book of the Law was found, covered with dust. The book was read to the young king. Upon hearing the Word, he knew his people had sinned. Josiah asked God for forgiveness. Josiah promised the Lord he would always remember Him.

You can read this story in 2 Chronicles, chapters 34 and 35!

Remember Your Creator

Remember your Creator in the days of your youth,
And you will live a happy life! Amen!
Don't forget, don't forget,
To remember the Lord and His promises!
Don't forget, don't forget,
To remember the Lord and His promises!

Devotion: Don't Forget to Remember

Erin can be so forgetful sometimes. The other day, she had a flat tire on her bicycle. No problem! She knew how to fix it. She was almost finished when Mom called her inside for lunch. After lunch, she went back down to the garage to hop on her bike and off she went. But suddenly, the front wheel started wobbling. It came completely off the bicycle!

She had forgotten something very important. She had forgotten to tighten the nuts that hold the tire in place!

Memory is really a cool thing. It helps you to make the right choices. It helps you live your life with fewer difficulties. If you remember God's Word, you can act upon it and live a good life. If you forget about God, you can find yourself in terrible trouble. In all that you do, remember the Lord your Creator and His commands. Don't forget to remember the Creator this week!

♟ HIDE THE WORD

Remember your Creator in the days of your youth.
—Ecclesiastes 12:1

◉ SEEK THE LORD

Five Fingers of Thanks

When we remember something, we think about it.
And when we remember our Creator, we think about
the many miracles He has done. We think about the
marvelous things he has done for us. Hold your hand
in the air and make a fist. Now, think of one thing God
has done for you. When you have, raise one finger and
say it out loud. Repeat until you have raised all five
fingers! (Hint: Family, friends, life, . . .)

✝ PRAY TO GOD

Dear Lord, may I never forget all
that You have done for me. May
I always remember Your unfailing
love toward me—a love that gave
me life as a baby, that keeps me
safe right now, and sent Jesus
to save me for all eternity. May
I always remember You, my
Creator and Lord. Amen.

The LORD is my **Shepherd, I shall not be in want.**

Psalm 23:1

David the Shepherd Boy (around 1025 BC)

David learned how to be a shepherd when he was a small boy. He knew that sheep weren't very smart. In fact, they were pretty goofy animals. They needed to be led, or they would go the wrong way. They needed to be fed, because they couldn't find a good pasture by themselves. They needed a protector who cared about them, because they couldn't defend themselves. David learned that shepherds lead the sheep, feed the sheep, and take care of the sheep.

You can read this story in 1 Samuel 17:34–37!

The Lord Is My Shepherd

The Lord is, the Lord is my shepherd.
The Lord is, the Lord is my shepherd.
The Lord is, the Lord is my shepherd.
How about you?
Yes, He is!

Devotion: The Good Shepherd

It was almost midnight when the hiking group reached the river. They unloaded in a clearing next to the Appalachian Trail. Their guide, Mr. Evans, said they would set up camp there. In the morning, they would begin their adventure through Newfoundland Gap. Mr. Evans had been there before. He knew the way. He had the compass and map. He would lead them. And like sheep, they would gladly follow!

The Lord is like a shepherd. He knows your needs. And if you choose to follow Him, He will lead you. He will lead you in paths of righteousness. A path is not a freeway, so you may not see many others walking the same way you are. But He's the Good Shepherd. He knows what you need and the way that is best for you!

♀ HIDE THE WORD

The LORD is my shepherd,
I shall not be in want.
—Psalm 23:1

👁 SEEK THE LORD

Follow the Shepherd

Who is your shepherd? That's easy to answer. Just look at who you are following. If it's the crowd . . . bad choice. The crowd will usually lead you away from God. We should make up our minds to follow Jesus. He's the Good Shepherd!

Take a paper plate and, with a crayon or marker, write, "The Lord is my Shepherd" around the outside edge. Now draw a little lamb in the center. You might copy one found in this book. You can color the lamb or glue cotton balls all over him. Put the lamb in your room somewhere as a reminder that we are all like sheep, and the Lord is our Shepherd!

✝ PRAY TO GOD

Dear Lord, be my shepherd. Lead me to places You want me to go, and teach me what You would have me do. I need You to restore my soul when I am hurting. Walk with me, Lord, through troubled valleys so that I may dwell in Your house forever. Amen.

Give **Thanks** to the LORD, for he is good.

Psalm 136:1

The Ten Lepers (around AD 30)

Once, Jesus was on His way to Jerusalem. He met ten men who had leprosy. They cried out, "Jesus, Master, have pity on us!" (Luke 17:13). Jesus told them to go and show themselves to the priest. As they went, they were healed! But only one of the ten men came back to thank Jesus for what He had done. Jesus asked, "Were not all ten cleansed? Where are the other nine?" (Luke 17:17). Jesus blessed the one who said thank you.

You can read this story in Luke 17:11–19!

Give Thanks unto the Lord

Oh, give thanks to the Lord!
Oh, give thanks for He is good!
Lift up your praises; let all the children say,
Lift up your praises to the Lord today!
Oh, give thanks to the Lord!
Oh, give thanks for He is good!

Devotion: Be Thankful

The girls' gymnastics team was traveling in a small van to a competition. It was just beginning to snow, when suddenly, the engine began to sputter. To everyone's horror, the van just stopped. There they sat, broken down in the snow. A few minutes later, a truck driver pulled up behind the van. "Having trouble?" he asked. Then the man opened the hood, made some adjustments, and—*vrooom!* The engine started. In all of the excitement, the team forgot to say "thank you"— all except Cindy. She ran back to the man's truck and said, "Thanks, mister!" He smiled as he drove away.

From the time you were very small, you've probably been taught to say "thank you." But do you remember to thank the most important One of all? Let God know every day how thankful you are. Thank Him for His protection. Thank Him for the love He has shown to you. Thank Him for His goodness to you and your family. Offer a prayer of thanksgiving this very minute. He is a good God!

⚷ HIDE THE WORD

Give thanks to the LORD, for he is good.
—Psalm 136:1

👁 SEEK THE LORD

One-Minute Praise

The Lord loves to hear praise and worship. Yes, we can praise God with music, and we can worship Him in song. But praise and worship is more than a melody. It's a way of life. Praise begins inside the heart. We think about who God is and all He has done. Our praise may lead us to say, "Thank You for loving me."

Praise and worship go hand in hand. Worship is praise in action. While looking at a clock, see how many things you can praise God for in one minute. Ready . . . go! (Hint: Life, health, home, . . .) If you can think of twenty items of praise in one minute, that would be awesome!

✝ PRAY TO GOD

Dear Lord, I praise You with my mouth for all You have done for me. I say, "Thank You, Lord, for You are so good." I worship You with my heart by praying right now. For I know worship is showing You how much I love You. Prayer is showing You I believe! Amen.

U

Trust in the LORD with all your heart and lean not on your own **Understanding.**

Proverbs 3:5

Mary Trusts God (around 6 BC)

Mary was confused. Nothing the angel had said to her made sense. She was engaged to a man named Joseph, but they weren't married yet. How could she be having a baby? She didn't understand. The angel had said to her, "Do not be afraid, Mary, you have found favor with God. You will be with child and give birth to a Son, and you are to give Him the name Jesus" (Luke 1:30–31). That's all Mary needed to hear. She answered, "I am the Lord's servant. . . . May it be to me as you have said" (Luke 1:38).

You can read the whole story in Luke 1:26–38!

Trust in the Lord

Trust in the Lord with all your heart,
And lean not on your own understanding.

Devotion: God Is in Control

Dylan buckled his seatbelt and looked out the window. It was the biggest engine he'd ever seen. This was his first airplane ride, and he was a little nervous. "How can this thing fly? Maybe we should get off," he told his mom. She leaned over and whispered to the passing flight attendant. The attendant smiled at Dylan and said, "Come with me." He walked with the attendant to the front of the plane. The pilot turned and said, "Welcome aboard! What can I do for you, young man?" Dylan spoke up, "How does the plane fly?" The pilot answered, "It's a little hard to understand, but trust me. I'll get you there safely. Just leave it to me." That's all Dylan needed to hear!

The Lord is like a pilot. And many times He simply says, "Trust Me. This will be very hard to understand, but I plan to get you there safely. Just leave it to Me." Can you trust Him? Because Mary trusted Him, a Savior was born who would later die to free the world from sin. You can trust God too! Even when you do not understand, trust Him—not your feelings. Lean on Him—not your understanding. And know that He is in control—not you. That's real trust!

⚷ HIDE THE WORD

Trust in the LORD with all your heart and lean not on your own understanding. —Proverbs 3:5

👁 SEEK THE LORD

Timber!

Sometimes life seems unfair. There are things that happen that we don't understand. Why do bad things happen the way they do? In those times, we must learn to trust God more. We must simply believe that all things are working for good, regardless of how they may seem. Now that's real trust and real faith! Have a parent stand behind you. Now fall backward and trust that your mom or dad will catch you. Ready? *T-I-M-B-E-R!* Learning to trust God is like that. He is always there to catch us should we fall!

✝ PRAY TO GOD

Dear God, so many times I cannot understand why things happen. But I know You always do. By faith, I believe that You are in control. So I rest knowing my confidence and trust is not in my own understanding. It is in You. Amen.

V

In the morning, O LORD, you hear my Voice.

Psalm 5:3

Joshua Calls on God (around 1400 BC)

Joshua knew he could call on God at any time. When great forces stood against Joshua and his army, he called out to God for help. God answered his call. He told Joshua, "Do not be afraid of them; I have given them into your hand" (Joshua 10:8). God confused the enemy, and Joshua and his men marched in and took them by surprise. With the power of God behind him, Joshua and his army defeated the mighty forces against them.

You can read the whole story in Joshua, chapter 10!

In the Morning I Will Hear Your Voice

In the morning, O Lord, You hear my voice.
In the morning, O Lord, You hear me call.
In the morning, O Lord, You hear my voice,
Praising who You are, saying,
Holy, holy You are!
Worthy, worthy You are!

Devotion: Let the Lord Hear Your Voice

Katy had just woken up from the scariest nightmare! She sat straight up in her bed and looked around in the darkness. "Mom?" she called in a scared voice. In seconds, her mom stood at her doorway, turned on the light, and came to Katy's side to comfort her. "I'm here. It's all right," she whispered. Katy's mom was right there when Katy called, even in the wee hours of the morning.

Many wake up each morning and never even think about the Lord. They go about their day with good health and blessings, never thinking of the One who has given it all to them. Let the Lord hear your voice. Let Him know you're thankful for all He's done in your life. When you get up and begin a new day, let God hear your voice, and take time to listen to His.

⚿ HIDE THE WORD

In the morning, O LORD, you hear my voice. —Psalm 5:3

👁 SEEK THE LORD

Morning Prayer

Morning is a very special time. It's like a new beginning! No matter what may have happened the day before, morning brings with it a fresh, new start. The old hymn says, "Morning by morning, new mercies I see." Tomorrow morning, start the day out right! When you wake up, kneel by your bed and let the Lord hear your voice, just the way He heard David's voice. Put a marker on this page so that in the morning, you can start your day by praying the prayer below out loud.

✝ PRAY TO GOD

Dear Lord, thank You for this beautiful new morning. I don't know what this day may bring, but I know that You will be with me, no matter what! I ask You to watch over all I do. I know that You hear my voice right now, just like You heard David's. So hear me say, "I love You, Lord," as I ask You to guide and direct me through this day You have made. Amen.

As for God, his **Way** is perfect; the word of the LORD is flawless.

2 Samuel 22:31

Jesus Is the Way (around AD 30)

Jesus once told His disciples that He was going to go and prepare a place for them. He said He would return and take them to where He was. He told them, "You know the way to the place where I am going" (John 14:4). Thomas asked, "Lord, we don't know where you are going, so how can we know the way?" Jesus answered, "I am the way and the truth and the life. No one comes to the Father except through me" (John 14:5-6).

You can read this story in John, chapter 14!

God's Way Is Perfect

Lots of ways to go,
Lots of ways you know.
As for God, His way is perfect.

Devotion: The One and Only Way

Ben and his dad just stared at the map, confused. Some roads followed along the shore. Some went to the shore and circled back into the mainland. But none went across to the tiny island. How could they get there? "Nobody gets to the island except by the ferry," the man at the gas station told them. So Ben and his dad bought their tickets for the ten o'clock ferry, and off they went. Sometimes, there's only one way to get there!

God's way isn't always the easy way, but it's the way to peace. God's way isn't always the short way, but it's the way home. God's way isn't always the fast way, but it is the right way. Jesus said, "I am the way." He's the only way! If you want to know and love God, you need to follow Jesus.

🔑 HIDE THE WORD

As for God, his way is perfect; the word of the LORD is flawless. —2 Samuel 22:31

◉ SEEK THE LORD

The Only Way

There are so many religions in the world today. And all but one of them have a founder who died and is buried somewhere. All but one! Only the Christian faith has a *living* Savior! Buddha is buried in Sri Lanka. Mohammed is buried in Saudi Arabia. But Jesus has no tomb. He is alive! That's why Jesus is now—and forever will be—the *only* way to the Father. He stands alone as Savior! Can you think of some other things that there is only *one* of? (Hint: God, snowflakes, and you!)

✝ PRAY TO GOD

Dear Father, I serve a living Savior—the only One! And You alone, Lord, sent Him into this world to pay the price for the sins of every single person. Because of Jesus—and Him alone— all people can come to You and worship You as Lord of all! Amen.

Glorify the LORD with me; let us eXalt his name together.

Psalm 34:3

Mary and Martha (around AD 29)

Mary and Martha were sisters. They both loved the Lord very much. But they chose different ways to show it. Martha served the Lord with her great service. Mary simply worshiped Him. One day, Jesus came to their home. Martha warmly welcomed Jesus and started preparing food. But Mary sat at Jesus' feet and worshiped Him. Martha felt like she was doing all the work. She said, "Lord, . . . tell her to help me!" (Luke 10:40). Jesus told Martha that Mary had her own way of worshiping. Both ways were good! Mary and Martha each used their own way to exalt the Lord.

You can read this story in Luke 10:38–42!

Glorify the Lord with Me

Glorify, glorify the Lord with me!
Glorify, glorify the Lord with me!
Let us exalt His name together!
Let us exalt His name forever!

Devotion: Glorify the Lord

The two brothers were as different as night and day. But they had one thing in common: they both wanted to make a Christmas gift for their mom. So Jason, the artistic one, decided to paint a picture. Chad, the practical one, decided to make a coupon book filled with chores he would do for his mother. They both loved their mother very much. They just had different ways of expressing it. Mom loved both gifts because she knew her sons were using their own special talents to give her a gift from their hearts.

People are very different in how they express their love for the Lord. Some glorify God with their service. They may help collect food for the hungry or empty the trash at church. Some sing; some play games with the children at Sunday school. In whatever you do, glorify the Lord, and proclaim His glory throughout the whole earth!

⚷ HIDE THE WORD

Glorify the LORD with me; let us exalt his name together. —Psalm 34:3

👁 SEEK THE LORD

Glorify the Lord

At the end of a movie, the names of the people who made the movie appear on the screen. It's called the "credits." It's very important that we, as believers, give God credit too—not for making a movie, but for making the world! The Bible calls it "glory"!

How can you give credit or glory to God? You can give Him glory by making known all that God has done. You can give Him credit for creating the heavens and the earth. They didn't just happen. If you like to sing, sing His glory! If you teach, teach His glory! If you write books, write His glory! Martha did it one way, and Mary another. But in everything you do, glorify the Lord!

✝ PRAY TO GOD

Dear Lord, I love You and want to glorify You with my life. May I always give You credit for all Your mighty deeds. May I always do the things that please You. May I show the world that You are worthy to be called Lord of all. Amen.

You are my hiding place; you will protect me from trouble.

Psalm 32:7

Hannah Made a Promise (around 1070 BC)

Hannah was married to a man named Elkanah. But she was unable to have children. Other mothers teased her until she cried and could not eat. She needed a hiding place. So Hannah went to the temple and fell before the Lord and prayed. She promised the Lord that if He gave her a son, she would give the child back to Him. Eli the priest blessed her before she went home. And in time, the Lord answered her prayer. Her son Samuel was born. Hannah had found comfort in the Lord. He was her hiding place.

You can read this story in 1 Samuel, chapter 1!

You Are My Hiding Place

You, You are my hiding place.
You will protect me from trouble all my days.
You, You are my hiding place.
You will protect me, O my Lord.

Devotion: God Will Protect You

Sometimes when you've had a really rough day, you'd like to find a hiding place. A place where no one can find you. A safe place where you can rest. A shelter from the storm. Maybe it's in a secret spot in your room that no one knows about. Or maybe in the branches of a tree in your yard. Everyone needs a hiding place sometimes.

The Lord is your hiding place. With Him you can feel safe from your enemies. You can feel secure. He will guard and protect you. If you are afraid, He calms you. If you are sad, He lifts you up. When you feel like you need a safe haven, don't run in panic. Run to your hiding place . . . the Lord.

♀ HIDE THE WORD

You are my hiding place; you will protect me from trouble. —Psalm 32:7

Hide and Seek

Let's play a game of Hide and Seek with a little different twist. You go hide. Then the others will come and look for you. But when they find you, the first to say, "The Lord is my hiding place!" will be the winner.

✝ PRAY TO GOD

Dear Lord, You are my hiding place. I run to You in times of trouble. I do this because I know that You will protect me. I can pour out my heart to You and know that You will keep me safe. Thank You, Father, for loving me and being my hiding place. Amen.

It is not good to have Zeal without knowledge.

Proverbs 19:2

Peter Had Great Zeal (around AD 30)

After Jesus finished praying in the Garden of Gethsemane, a mob came carrying torches and clubs. Led by Judas, they had come to take Jesus away. In his zeal, Peter took his sword and cut off the ear of one of the guards. "Put your sword away!" said Jesus (John 18:11). Then He reached out and healed the man's ear. Peter had great zeal, but he did not understand that this was God's plan for Jesus.

You can read this story in John, chapter 18!

It Is Not Good to Have Zeal without Knowledge

Zeal, zeal, zeal–
Without knowledge, it is not good to have.
Zeal, zeal, zeal–
Without knowledge, it is not good to have.

Devotion: Think Before You Act

Sheila had never had any training. In fact, she'd never been ice-skating in her life. But how hard could it be? Put on the skates and glide across the ice. Easy! As Sheila and her parents approached the ice, she watched a couple twirling and spinning in the center of the rink. So she jumped onto the ice and . . . went slipping and sliding out of control! Again and again, she tried. Again and again, she ended up sprawled on all fours. As much as she wanted to twirl and spin on the ice, she just didn't have the training to do it.

To do things the right way, you must have the desire and the knowledge to do it. If you desire to play the piano, you must have knowledge of music to play beautiful melodies. To act without knowledge can be very dangerous and embarrassing. In the Garden of Gethsemane, Peter acted without knowledge. He did not know that God had a bigger plan . . . a plan of salvation. Think before you act!

⚷ HIDE THE WORD

It is not good to have zeal without knowledge.
—Proverbs 19:2

◉ SEEK THE LORD

Tongue Twister

Have you ever attempted to do something you thought was very easy, only to jump in and find it very hard to do? Maybe you think you can read the next sentence without a mistake. Do you think you can? Are you sure? OK . . . here we go! "The sixth sick shepherd's sixth sheep's sick." Did you do it? Now say it six times, faster each time! Maybe you just experienced what the writer of Proverbs called "zeal without knowledge"! It's always best to be sure before you say you can do something.

✝ PRAY TO GOD

Dear Lord, sometimes I jump in too fast, thinking I can do something, but then I fail. I don't always know what You want me to do. Please help me wait on Your instruction before doing something I will regret. May I always think before I act. Amen.

a

And we know that in **all** things God works for the good of those who love him.

Romans 8:28

The Crucifixion of Jesus (around AD 30)

Jesus knew that all things work together for good—even when He was hung on the cross to die. Although it was the saddest day ever, Jesus knew that something good was about to happen. He knew the world would soon be rejoicing. And three days later, all things *did* work together for good. He arose! And the sins of all who love Him were forgiven.

You can read this story in the book of Matthew, chapter 27:32–28; Mark, chapters 15 and 16; and Luke, chapters 23 and 24!

And We Know That in All Things

And we know that in all things,
God works for the good of those who love Him.
And we know that in all things,
God works for the good of those who love Him.

Devotion: Keep Trusting

Have you ever had to work very hard for something you wanted really badly? Practicing for a recital can be tiring! Studying for a test can be brain-bending! Learning to ride a bike can be painful! But you keep on trying, because you know something good is going to come from all that hard work. Then, when you finally play your song perfectly, ace the test, or zoom around the block on your bike, you know it was all worth it.

God has given us a promise: all things will work together for the good of those who love Him. So no matter what happens, keep trusting in Jesus! He loves you so much that He died to save you. He will work for the good in your life.

🔑 HIDE THE WORD

And we know that in all things God works for the good of those who love him.
—Romans 8:28

Good or Bad?

A lot of people think that "good things" have to be "fun things." But the Bible has a different view. It wasn't fun for Daniel to be put in a lions' den. But God used that lions' den for good. What happened? The people of Persia came to know the Lord because of Daniel! That's good! The Bible defines a "good thing" as something that brings glory to God. Can you think of some other Bible characters whose bad situations brought about good? (Hint: A whale, a fire, and a shipwreck.)

✝ PRAY TO GOD

Dear Lord, as You work out Your plan for my life, please help me know that good things aren't always "fun things." May I always remember that all things are working together for the good of those who love You. May I trust You as Daniel did, whether things are fun or not so fun. Amen.

Answers: Jonah; Shadrach, Meshach, and Abednego; Paul

How **beautiful** are the feet of those who bring good news!

Romans 10:15

Paul Was a Missionary (around AD 55)

Paul was a missionary. Missionaries can travel far to tell others about Jesus. When Paul traveled to many different places, he would usually walk. Wherever he walked, he told everyone the Good News about God's love. They called his message beautiful. And since his feet brought him there, they called his feet beautiful too! His feet brought the beautiful message of God's grace.

You can read about how Paul became a missionary in the book of Acts, chapter 9!

How Beautiful Are the Feet of Those Who Bring Good News

How beautiful are the feet
Of those who bring Good News!
How beautiful are the feet
Of those who bring Good News!

Devotion: A Beautiful Message

God has made so many beautiful things. He made the beautiful oceans with their soft, curling waves. He made the big, beautiful blue skies where birds can soar. He gave people beautiful voices to sing praises to Him. But have you heard of beautiful feet? The Bible says that those who bring the Good News of Jesus to others have "beautiful feet"!

You don't have to travel far to find someone who has not heard about Jesus. Many of your friends may have never heard the Good News of God's love. So wherever you go, be sure to tell everyone about Jesus. Your message will be a beautiful message. And the feet that brought you will be beautiful too!

⚷ HIDE THE WORD

How beautiful are the feet of those who bring good news! —Romans 10:15

👁 SEEK THE LORD

Wiggle Your Toes

Let's pull off our shoes and socks right now. Go ahead! There they are . . . two little feet and ten wiggly toes. They may look like ordinary feet to you. But when your feet take you to where you can tell others about God's love, those feet become beautiful feet! Is there someone you know who needs to hear about God's love? Just say with me, "My feet are beautiful!" Then go and tell them about Jesus . . . but please, wear your shoes!

✝ PRAY TO GOD

Dear Lord, I want my feet to be beautiful! I want to use them to go and tell others about Your love. Then my whole life will be beautiful to You and to those who come to Jesus. Thank You for the beautiful message of Your love. Amen.

Let the little **children** come to me.

Matthew 19:14

Jesus and the Children (around AD 30)

Jesus thought children were very important. He always had time for them. Once, His disciples thought He was too busy to meet the children. But when Jesus saw their eager smiles, He said, "Let the little children come to me . . . for the kingdom of heaven belongs to such as these" (Matthew 19:14). Jesus loves children!

You can read this story in Matthew, chapter 19!

Let the Little Children Come to Me

Let 'em, won't you let 'em?
Let the little children come to Me.
Let 'em, won't you let 'em?
Let the little children come to Me.

Devotion: You Are Awesome

Sometimes being a kid can feel less important than being a grown-up. You're too young to drive a car. You're too little to ride the Dashin' Dragon roller coaster at the park. And grown-ups are always saying, "Be quiet!" or "Not now!" or "Hurry up!" It's tough being a kid!

But children are important to God! Jesus wants children everywhere to know about His special love for them. What you learn as a child will stay with you as you grow up, giving you many years to learn from and grow closer to God. Jesus thinks you are awesome! So have a great day being an awesome child of the best Father of all—God!

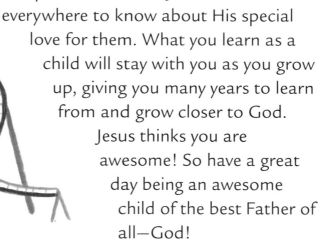

♞ HIDE THE WORD

Let the little children come to me.
—Matthew 19:14

👁 SEEK THE LORD

Special Invitation

There's nothing better than getting a special invitation to a party! When you get an invitation, you probably can't wait to get there and see all your friends. Guess what? You've been given a special invitation. It's found in Matthew 19:14. Jesus has given kids everywhere a very special invitation to come and be with Him. His kingdom is not just for grown-ups . . . it's for kids too!

Maybe you can make a special invitation card and invite someone you know to go to church with you this Sunday. Give them a special invitation, just like Jesus did!

✝ PRAY TO GOD

Dear Lord, I am special. I am special because You love me. I'm special because You hear my prayers and answer me. I am special because I'm a kid, and You love kids like me. Thank You, Lord, for making me special. Amen.

Do to others what you would have them do to you.

Matthew 7:12

Joseph and His Brothers (around 1900 BC)

Joseph's older brothers did not treat him the way they wanted to be treated. They were jealous of Joseph and decided to do a terrible thing. They tricked him and sold him to an Egyptian merchant. He was taken to Egypt, far away from his home in Israel. Years later, when a famine came to Israel, Joseph's brothers went to Egypt to buy food. Guess who was in charge of the food? That's right: Joseph! But he did not return their unkindness. He loved them and took care of them.

You can read the whole story in Genesis, chapters 37 to 45!

Do to Others What You Would Have Them Do to You

Do, do to others what you
Would have them do to you, to you.
Do, do to others what you
Would have them do to you, to you.

Devotion: The Golden Rule

It takes real courage to be nice. If you were the only person living on the planet, you wouldn't have to worry about being nice. There would be no one to disagree with you. You wouldn't have to be patient. You wouldn't have to share with anyone. But look around. There are seven billion people on this planet. So, you have to be able to get along with others. The best way to do that is to treat others the way you want to be treated.

Treating others the way you would like to be treated is called the "Golden Rule." It is golden because of its great value. It creates a world where people of all races and nationalities can live in peace together. It's also golden because those who follow the rule will shine like gold. Starting today, try to treat others just like you want them to treat you!

🔑 HIDE THE WORD

Do to others what you would have them do to you.
—Matthew 7:12

◉ SEEK THE LORD

The Golden List

Now that you've learned the Golden Rule, we're going to make a Golden List. Get a pencil and paper, and write down three things you would like people to always do to you. For example: I would like my big brother to always treat me nicely; I would like my friends to share with me. Now, see if you can do the things on your list. Treat others the way you would like to be treated!

✝ PRAY TO GOD

Dear Lord, the Golden Rule is easy to say, but hard to do. Help me to care about others the way Jesus cares about me. May I always treat others the way I want to be treated. Amen.

Everyone who calls on the name of the Lord will be saved.

Romans 10:13

Jesus Heals the Blind Man (around AD 30)

One day Jesus was passing through Jericho. A blind man heard the noise of the crowds and wondered what was happening. He could not see. His friends told him that Jesus had come to Jericho. The blind man knew he needed help if he was ever going to see. He shouted, "Jesus . . . have mercy on me!" (Luke 18:38). Jesus heard the blind man calling His name. Jesus answered and healed him. The blind man could see!

You can read this story in Luke, chapter 18!

Everyone Who Calls on the Name of the Lord

Everyone, everyone, everyone,
Who calls on the name of the Lord,
They will be saved forever.
Everyone who calls,
Everyone who calls,
On the name of the Lord.

Devotion: Call Upon the Lord

If you saw an accident and needed to get help fast, who would you call? Would you call the pizza delivery man? Or the plumber? Of course not! You'd call 9-1-1 and get the emergency medical team on its way. There may be days when you feel bad or sad or upset. That's when you need to remember who to call: call upon the Lord!

It is very important to know who to call when you need help. The blind man knew that only Jesus could give him sight, so he called upon the name of the Lord. He was saved from his blindness. You can call upon the name of the Lord and be saved from danger, bullies, temptation, and even your own sin. He will help you today. Just call on Him!

⚷ HIDE THE WORD

Everyone who calls on the name of the Lord will be saved. —Romans 10:13

My One-Second Prayer

Knowing who to call in an emergency is very important. Here are three letters and three numbers I want you to remember: G-O-D and 9-1-1. First, call G-O-D. Call upon the Lord with this prayer: "Lord, help us!" It only takes one second to pray this prayer! Next, if it's a real emergency, call 9-1-1.

Let's make a colorful reminder. Get out some crayons and paper. Divide the page into four boxes. In box 1, draw a fire. In box 2, draw a police car. In box 3, draw a hospital. In box 4, draw a wrecker truck. At the top of the page, write "Call G-O-D." At the bottom, write "Call 9-1-1." Both are very important calls!

✝ PRAY TO GOD

Dear God, I want You to always be my *first* response in times of trouble, not my last resort. If fire breaks out, may I call on You as Shadrach, Meshach, and Abednego did. If there is trouble, may I call on You as Jonah did. Teach me to call upon the mighty name of the Lord first, and You will help me know what to do! Amen.

Forgive as the Lord forgave you.

Colossians 3:13

Peter Learns to Forgive (around AD 29)

Peter once came to Jesus. He wanted to learn to forgive. So he asked Jesus, "How many times shall I forgive my brother when he sins against me? Up to seven times?" (Matthew 18:21). Jesus told Peter that he should forgive more than seven times. He should forgive seven times seventy! Jesus explained that there was no limit to God's forgiveness, so Peter should have no limit to his forgiveness for others.

You can read the whole story in Matthew, chapter 18!

We Learn to Live When We Forgive

Forgive a little bit, gonna be like Jesus!
Forgive a little bit, gonna be like Him!
Forgive a little bit, never gonna quit livin' for Him!
Forgive a little bit, as the Lord forgave you!
Forgive a little bit, gonna be like Him!
We learn to live when we forgive, we forgive.

Devotion: Forgive Others

It is always important to treat others with kindness. That seems like an easy thing to do, right? Well, it is easy until someone is mean to you. That's when you have to make a choice. Do you return meanness for meanness? Do you hold a grudge? No! There's a better choice. You can learn to forgive!

If there is ever a time that someone treats you unfairly, remember the lesson Peter learned from Jesus. Forgive that person as the Lord forgave you. Think about the many times you have been forgiven by your heavenly Father. Then choose to act like Jesus. Forgive!

🔑 HIDE THE WORD

Forgive as the Lord forgave you. —Colossians 3:13

Rocks in a Box

Imagine your heart to be an empty box. Every time you sin, it's like placing a heavy rock inside that box. Without Jesus, your heart becomes weighed down and full of sin. But when you receive Jesus as your Savior, you are forgiven! He takes away the sin, like taking away heavy rocks from your box. Because of Jesus, you're forgiven and your burden is light!

† PRAY TO GOD

Dear Lord, I know that there is no limit to Your forgiveness. You taught Peter to forgive. I must learn to forgive too. As You have removed the "rocks of sin" from  my heart, may I learn to forgive others who have sinned against me. Amen.

Give, and it will be given to you.

Luke 6:38

Jesus Feeds Thousands (around AD 29)

Jesus once made a *lot* from a little offering. He was preaching on a hillside to five thousand people. When evening came, the people were very hungry, but there was no food. One boy offered his lunch of five barley loaves and two small fish to Jesus. But how far would that go to feed so many? Jesus blessed the loaves and fish. Then five thousand people ate dinner and had as much as they wanted. It was a great miracle!

You can read the whole story in John, chapter 6!

Jesus Said, "Give"

Jesus said, "Give, and it will be given to you."
Jesus said, "Give, and it will be given to you."
We must understand
That a little in God's hand
Is truly better than
A lot in our own.

Devotion: A Happy Giver

Keisha looked at the offering plate. It was coming her way. She reached in her purse and pulled out a quarter. She wanted to give more than that! The plate was full of dollars, checks, and envelopes stuffed with money. She just had twenty-five cents, but she gave it all. Keisha wondered, *What can God do with my little offering?*

A little in God's hands is better than a lot in your own hands. He has promised in the Bible that if you are willing to give unselfishly to others, He is willing to give back to you an even greater blessing. Imagine a blessing so big that your house wouldn't be able to hold it. It's nice to know that you can never "out-give" God! Be a happy giver!

🔑 HIDE THE WORD

Give, and it will be given to you. —Luke 6:38

👁 SEEK THE LORD

A Giving Tree

Let's learn to give by making a Giving Chain. Ask an adult to help you cut strips of paper and write something you might be able to give on each strip. (Hint: a toy, a meal, time, money, or help.) Each time you are blessed to give, remove a link from your Giving Chain. See how long it takes for you to get to the end—and remember, you can always start again!

✝ PRAY TO GOD

Dear Lord, I know I can't out-give You. You have given me life and love. All that I have is a blessing from You. The little boy gave his lunch, and You made it a banquet. May I learn to give my all to You and watch as You multiply it a thousand times! Amen.

The Lord is my helper; I will not be afraid.

Hebrews 13:6

Daniel in the Lions' Den (around 539 BC)

Daniel had a big problem. The king had made a law that everyone had to pray to him and only him. But Daniel would only pray to God—not to a person! When Daniel refused to pray to the king, he was thrown into a den of hungry lions. All alone, Daniel was no match for those hungry lions. But the Lord was with him. Daniel called out for help, and God shut the mouths of the lions. Daniel was saved!

You can read the whole story in Daniel, chapter 6!

The Lord Is My Helper

The Lord is my helper.
The Lord is my helper.
The Lord is my helper.
I will not be afraid.

Devotion: No Problem!

Everyone needs help at one time or another. Sometimes a problem is just too big for one person to solve. Sometimes a burden is just too heavy to carry alone. That's when you need a helper, someone who loves you and cares about you. What can you do when you need help with a problem?

God loves you and cares about you all the time. You are never out of His sight. You are always in His hands. So when trouble comes, remember: you are not alone. Call on the Lord. There is no burden too heavy for Him, no problem He cannot solve. Problems can be big; problems can be small. But any problem in God's hands is no problem at all!

☦ HIDE THE WORD

The Lord is my helper; I will not be afraid. —Hebrews 13:6

👁 SEEK THE LORD

Invisible Helper

Sailboats have an "invisible helper." Can you guess what it is? The wind! You can't see the wind, but it's there, day after day, helping sailboats move across the water.

How helpful can you be? Lay a paper cup on its side. Without touching it, blow into the open end of the cup using a drinking straw. The air is invisible, but it moves the cup! God is like the wind. You can't see God, but He's always there; our invisible friend moving in our lives. He's our invisible helper.

✝ PRAY TO GOD

Dear Lord, You are invisible, and yet You are more real and more powerful than the mighty wind. Thank You, Lord, for being my helper. I can rest knowing that You will be my invisible helper each and every day. Amen.

What is **impossible** with men is possible with God.

Luke 18:27

Sarah Receives a Miracle (around 2066 BC)

Sarah received a miracle. She was the wife of Abraham. God had promised them a son. He told Abraham that his descendents would outnumber the stars in the sky. But many years had passed, and Abraham was now 100 years old. When the Lord told Abraham it was time to have a son, Sarah laughed. *Impossible*, she thought. *We're too old!* But one year later, a little baby boy was born. Their impossible dream was named Isaac.

You can read the whole story in Genesis 18!

What Is Impossible with Men Is Possible with God

What is impossible with men,
Is possible with God!
No matter what the odds may be,
In Christ I find my victory!
What is impossible with men,
Is possible with God, my friend!

Devotion: God Can!

The doctors came out of the operating room with their heads lowered. They had worked very hard to remove the cancer. The family walked quietly into the hospital room and knelt beside little Zach's bed to pray. "Lord, the doctors said only a miracle can heal him now. We ask You, Lord, to do what is impossible for us to do." The Lord answered their prayers, and Zach got well. He received a miracle!

Is anything too hard for the Lord? Whether it's healing the sick or keeping His promise that a baby will be born, God can do it! Let these words encourage you: My God can! He can do what no man can do. All things are possible in the hands of Almighty God.

🔑 HIDE THE WORD

What is impossible with men is possible with God.
—Luke 18:27

👁 SEEK THE LORD

Only God Can Do It!

We used to think it was impossible to fly. Then came the airplane. We thought it was impossible to talk to someone a thousand miles away. Then came the telephone. Though these inventions are amazing, there are still things only God can do. Can you think of three things only God can do? (Hint: The universe, man and animals, salvation.)

✝ PRAY TO GOD

Dear Lord, only You can draw people to Yourself. Only You can show me the truth. Only You can make me sorry for my sins. Thank You, Lord, for doing the impossible. Thank You for sending Jesus. Without Him, it would be impossible for me to reach heaven. Amen.

Answers: Only God can create the stars and planets; only God can create animals and man; God's Son is the only way to salvation.

Jesus answered, . . . "You must be born again."

John 3:5–7

Nicodemus (around AD 27)

Nicodemus had heard Jesus teach. He had seen the miracles Jesus had done. But when Jesus spoke of being born again, Nicodemus was confused. "How can a man be born when he is old?" Nicodemus asked. Jesus explained that he was speaking of a spiritual birth. Just as we are born physically, we must also be born spiritually if we want to enter heaven. This happens when we say no to sin, turn from it, and say yes to Jesus. Remember, no one can enter the kingdom of heaven unless he is born again.

Read about Nicodemus in John, chapter 3!

Jesus Said, "You Must Be Born Again"

Jesus said, "You must be born again."
Gonna ask Him into my heart!
Gonna ask Him today, ask Him to stay!
Gonna ask Him to be the Lord of me!

Devotion: Born Again

One summer day, Shelby and her family headed to the amusement park. As they reached the ticket booth, the man behind the counter waved Shelby and her little sister through. But he stopped their parents at the gate. "I'm sorry," he said, "but to enter, you must turn into a child." Shelby's mom and dad exchanged confused looks. "But sir," Mom began, "we're adults. There's no way we can turn back into children." The man burst into laughter. "I don't mean your age. Only the young at heart can enter here!" Shelby's parents looked at each other again and smiled. "Oh, we can be like children," they said. And they entered the gates.

How can you be born again? When you ask Jesus to come into your heart, you are born again spiritually. And as babies depend on their parents, you will then depend on your heavenly Father. When you get hungry, the Bible will encourage you. When you are weak, God will make you strong. You will be a new person. You will be born again. And you will be able to enter the kingdom of God!

🔑 HIDE THE WORD

Jesus answered, . . . "You must be born again."
—John 3:5–7

👁 SEEK THE LORD

Get out of the Dark Room

When you were born the first time, you did a very amazing thing: you traded spaces. You moved out of a place that was dark and very cramped, and started a new "life" in a great big beautiful world of love and light! When we are born again, we do the very same thing, only with our heart. We move out of a place of darkness, where people do not know Jesus, and we start a new "life" in God's wonderful kingdom of light! We do this by giving our heart to Jesus!

Before you go to bed tonight, close the door and turn off the light. Wait a few minutes. Name everything you can see. It's hard to see anything in the dark! Now, open your bedroom door and walk into a room full of light. What do you see? Everything! Being born again is like moving from a dark room to a room full of light.

✝ PRAY TO GOD

Dear Lord, once a baby is born it can never go back to its mother's womb. It's now in the care of loving parents. Lord, You are my loving heavenly Father. I want to trust You more. I want to be born again by moving from where I am to where You want me to be: in the arms of Jesus. Amen.

k

Always try to be **kind** to each other and to everyone else.

1 Thessalonians 5:15

Ruth and Naomi (between 1210 BC and 1050 BC)

Ruth and her mother-in-law, Naomi, lived together in a place far from Naomi's home. Both Naomi's and Ruth's husbands had died. One day, Naomi decided that it was time to return to her homeland. But Ruth loved Naomi and did not want her to go alone. Ruth knew exactly what to do. She told Naomi, "Every place you go, I will go" (Ruth 1:16 ICB). Ruth left her home and traveled many miles to Judah to be with Naomi. God soon blessed Ruth for her kindness to Naomi. There Ruth met a man named Boaz, and they were married.

You can read the whole story in the book of Ruth!

Always Try to Be Kind

Always, always try to be kind.
Always, always try to be kind.
To each other, sister and brother,
To everyone, to everyone else,
Be kind.

Devotion: A Spirit of Kindness

It was Marcia's first day at school. She had moved from Costa Rica and spoke very little English. She was nervous and quite shy. As class ended, Marcia stood alone. One girl walked over and said, "Hi, Marcia. My name is Wendy. Welcome to our school!" Marcia's face lit up with a bright, beautiful smile. "Thank you," she answered. Marcia and Wendy began to talk, and before long, Marcia had invited Wendy over to swim in her pool!

Sometimes God whispers to your heart, "Say a kind word to the visitor," or "Go visit the elderly lady across the street." Being kind is a choice we make. It is also one of the fruits of the Spirit mentioned in the Bible. When you pray, ask God to give you a spirit of kindness. Then treat it like peanut butter—spread it around!

⚷ HIDE THE WORD

Always try to be kind to each other and to everyone else.
—1 Thessalonians 5:15

◉ SEEK THE LORD

The Kindness Game

How can we demonstrate kindness to others? Here's an idea. Play "The Kindness Game." Get a few of your friends together and form a circle. Toss a ball to someone and say something kind to the one who catches it. (Hint: Jesus loves you; you're a good friend; or I like your smile.) Being kind can be lots of fun!

✝ PRAY TO GOD

Dear Lord, You have asked me to be kind to others. It's easy when people are kind to me, but it's hard when they are not. Teach me again that kindness is a choice I make. Help me, Lord to choose kindness, even when others are unkind to me. Amen.

For God so **loved** the world that he gave his one and only Son, that whoever believes in him shall not perish but have eternal life.

John 3:16

God So Loved the World (The book of John was written between AD 80 and AD 90. Christ was crucified in the Spring of AD 30.)

God said "I love you" to the whole world. And He did it in a very special way. Your loving God—whose power has no limits, whose strength cannot be measured—your God who knows all things, gave a very special gift to you. He gave His one and only Son, Jesus, to die on the cross. Because of that gift, your sins can be forgiven, and you can have eternal life!

You can read about this in John, chapter 3!

For God So Loved the World

For God so loved the world,
For God so loved the world,
For God so loved the world,
That He gave His one and only Son.

Devotion: The Greatest Gift of All

When you love somebody, you want to make that person happy. Giving a gift is a great way to make someone happy. When you spend your time, money, or effort to create a gift for someone, you show that you really care. A gift says "I love you" in a special way.

There are many kinds of gifts, big and small. Some have great value. God's gift to you has a greater value than anyone could ever imagine—a gift of eternal life. This gift allows you to live forever in heaven. But it came at a great cost. It cost Jesus His life. Receive this gift with great joy. It's God's gift of love to the world—and to you!

🔑 HIDE THE WORD

For God so loved the world that he gave his one and only Son, that whoever believes in him shall not perish but have eternal life. —John 3:16

3:16 Love

How big is the world? Very big! It's a giant rotating ball that's over 24,000 miles around. Seven billion people are rotating with it, and God loves every one of them. No matter where they are, you can help reach out to them with 3:16 Love. Here's how! See if you can earn $3.16 over the next few days. Use your allowance money, or maybe help your mom or a neighbor with some extra chores. Put the money in an envelope and give it to the missions fund at your church. Label it 3:16 Love. God loves all the people of the world, so let's show them some 3:16 Love this week!

✝ PRAY TO GOD

Dear Lord, John 3:16 says that You loved the world so much You sent Your Son. Thank You for Your wonderful gift of 3:16 Love. Thank You for sending Jesus. I believe that Jesus died for me and rose again. And because He lives, I'll live forever in heaven. Amen.

Be **merciful**, just as your Father is merciful.

Luke 6:36

The Unmerciful Servant (around AD 28)

Jesus spoke of a servant who asked for mercy. He owed the king a lot of money, but he could not pay the debt. The servant begged for mercy, "Be patient . . . and I will pay back everything" (Matthew 18:26). The king showed great mercy and forgave the servant's debt. But that same servant found another man who owed him money. He, too, begged for mercy. But no mercy was shown. The servant had the man who was in debt to him thrown into prison. When the king heard what the evil servant had done, he was very angry.

You can read this story in Matthew, chapter 18!

Be Merciful

Be merciful, be merciful, be merciful,
Just as your Father is merciful.
Be merciful, be merciful, be merciful,
Just as your Father is merciful.

Devotion: Live Like Jesus

Brittany had worked so hard on her homework assignment. How could she have left for school without it? It was due today, and it counted as half of her grade. She was nearly in tears when she walked up to her teacher's desk. "Mr. Rhymer, I'm sorry, but I forgot my homework. I really did it, and I worked so hard." Mr. Rhymer forgave her and said, "You've been a wonderful student, Brittany. Could you bring it tomorrow?"

Justice is getting what you deserve. Mercy is getting something good that you do not deserve. We can learn to show mercy by doing the thing Jesus did. He had mercy upon the sick, the dying, even you. Everyone who sins deserves death. But because of Jesus, you are given mercy. Sometimes, the thing you don't deserve is the thing you need the most!

⚷ HIDE THE WORD

Be merciful, just as your Father is merciful.
—Luke 6:36

The Mercy Message

Giving a precious gift to someone who doesn't deserve it seems unfair. People should earn what they get, right? Not so fast! Lots of things can be earned, like money or a high school diploma. But mercy isn't earned. Mercy is getting something you did not earn and do not deserve. Written below in secret code is a Mercy Message. To solve it, let the letter A=1, the letter B=2, the letter C=3, and so on. Now decode the following message:

__ __ __ __ __ __ __ __ __ __!
2 5   13 5 18 3 9 6 21 12

✝ PRAY TO GOD

Dear Lord, have mercy on me. I do not deserve all the good You shower on me, yet You bless me with Your love and watchful care. Teach me to be merciful as You, my Father, are merciful. Amen.

Answer: Be merciful!

n Love your **neighbor** as yourself.

Matthew 19:19

The Good Samaritan (around AD 28)

Jesus once told a parable about a man traveling from Jerusalem to Jericho. The man was robbed, beaten, and left lying on the side of the road. A passing priest saw the man, but did nothing to help him. Next, another helper from the church passed by, but he, too, did nothing. Then came a Samaritan. He stopped and cared for the man. He bandaged his wounds and took him to an inn and even paid for the room himself. After Jesus told the story, He asked, "Which of these three do you think was a neighbor . . . ?" (Luke 10:36). Surely it was the one who met the needs of the hurting!

You can read the whole story in Luke, chapter 10!

Love Your Neighbor

Love your neighbor.
Love your neighbor as yourself.
Love your neighbor.
Love your neighbor as yourself.

Devotion: Be a Good Neighbor

Rosa had never seen snow falling the way it did on that day. She tried to catch snowflakes on her tongue as she walked with her dad toward the mall. As they made their last turn, Rosa saw a homeless man huddled on the sidewalk. He had no coat. Without saying a word, her father took off his coat and covered the man. Then he said, "I'll pay for your room tonight at that motel," pointing across the street. Rosa has never forgotten that moment.

So, who is your neighbor? Your neighbor is anyone who has a need that you can meet. You don't have to look very hard to find people with needs. Perhaps in your own family, school, or church, you know someone who could use a visit or a cheerful word. Just think: if you love your neighbor as yourself, God can change the entire neighborhood!

⚷ HIDE THE WORD

Love your neighbor as yourself. —Matthew 19:19

👁 SEEK THE LORD

Being a Good Neighbor

Who is your neighbor? Anyone who has a need. Perhaps there is someone in your church or community who could use a good neighbor. Maybe they need warm clothing. Perhaps they are hungry or without a home. Talk to your parents or your pastor, and see what you and your church family can do to be a good neighbor!

✝ PRAY TO GOD

Dear Lord, I am blessed to be a blessing to others. Help me see the needs all around me, Father. Help me respond in love. May I always be a good neighbor as Jesus commanded. Amen.

Children, **obey** your parents in the Lord.

Ephesians 6:1

Jonah and the Whale (around 785 BC)

Poor Jonah had to learn to obey the hard way. God told Jonah to go to Nineveh and preach. Jonah didn't want to, so he sailed the other way. God sent a terrible storm, which tossed the big ship up and down. Jonah knew the storm was his fault. He told the sailors, "Throw me into the sea . . . and it will become calm" (Jonah 1:12). Jonah was tossed overboard and . . . *gulp!* He was swallowed by a great big fish. For three days, Jonah was inside the belly of that fish as it swam through the ocean. He promised God, "I will obey this time." The fish spit him out on dry land. Jonah finally obeyed and went to Nineveh!

You can read the whole story in the book of Jonah!

Children, Obey Your Parents in the Lord

Children, obey your parents in the Lord,
For this is right. Honor your father and mother,
Which is the first commandment with a promise.

Devotion: Learning to Obey

Tasha didn't always obey the first time she was told to do something. Many times, her mother would have to ask two or three times before she would obey. One day, she and her mother were kicking a soccer ball in the front yard. With one kick, it rolled into the street. Without paying attention to the passing car, Tasha ran into the street. "Tasha, stop!" her mother shouted. *Honk! Screech!* The car barely missed hitting her! Tasha was almost hurt because she did not obey her mother the first time.

Learning to obey the first time is a very good habit. Jonah spent three very unpleasant days inside a big fish because he did not obey his heavenly Father the first time. Learning to obey your parents is a very important sign of growing up. Your parents have wisdom, and God has said in His Word that you should obey your parents. God has all wisdom so you should trust and obey Him—the first time!

⚷ HIDE THE WORD

Children, obey your parents in the Lord. —Ephesians 6:1

God's Recipe

Recipes are like easy-to-follow rules. If you follow the rules and do exactly what the recipe says, you will enjoy something yummy. If you don't, it may not taste so good. With your mom's help, let's make some Kool-Aid, but let's break one of the rules. We won't add any sugar. Here we go! Mix it up and taste it. The Kool-Aid is bitter because we disobeyed the rules. Life is like that. Life is full and sweet only when we follow God's recipe! It's called obedience.

✝ PRAY TO GOD

Dear Lord, sometimes Your laws may seem like a burden. They seem to spoil all the fun. But help me to remember that obedience to Your commands makes life sweet. It has great benefits, for You bless those who love You and obey Your commands. Amen.

Be **patient**, bearing with one another in love.

Ephesians 4:2

The Prodigal Son (around AD 28)

Jesus tells of a patient father who loved his two sons dearly. The younger one said, "Give me my share of the family inheritance now. I'm leaving for a far country." The loving father did as his son had asked. The son moved away and soon wasted all of his money. He became so hungry that he took a job feeding pigs and even ate their food. One day, he came to his senses. *I'll go home and work for my father,* he thought. When he was almost home, his patient father ran to him and hugged him. The boy said, "I am no longer worthy to be called your son. May I work for you?" But his father loved him and celebrated his return!

You can read this story in Luke, chapter 15!

Be Patient

You've planted a seed in a garden today.
Be patient, for this we do know.
You've planted a seed. Now there's coming a day.
Be patient, the flower will grow.

Devotion: Good Things Take Time

Matt really didn't mean to do it. He had one hand on the glass, one hand on the door. But when Sparky barked and came bounding through the door—*splash!*—milk went everywhere. Mom grabbed a handful of paper towels and said patiently, "It's just a little spill. It's okay." Together, Mom and Matt cleaned up the milk.

A big part of loving someone is showing patience. Sometimes, you have to put up with things you don't like. No one plants a seed of corn in the ground and comes back the next day asking, "Where's the corn?" You must be patient. Good things take a little time. Today, practice a little patience with your family and friends.

HIDE THE WORD

Be patient, bearing with one another in love.
—Ephesians 4:2

👁 SEEK THE LORD

Patient Toast

The Bible says in one short sentence that love is patient (1 Corinthians 13:4). But learning to be patient takes a lifetime. Here is a beginner's exercise in patience. With your mom or dad close by, place a piece of bread in the toaster. Count to three then pop it up. Is it crispy? Why not? You weren't patient. It takes more than three seconds! Put the bread back in the toaster and wait until the toaster pops it up. Your patience will get the result you want: toast!

Being patient with yourself and others always brings about a more positive outcome. It is what we should do. It's what God expects.

✝ PRAY TO GOD

Dear Father, You have promised eternal life to those who trust in Jesus. I do, Lord. I trust in Jesus, so I will live forever. And since I am going to live forever, help me be patient with myself and with others in the days and years ahead. I have plenty of time! Amen.

q

Everyone should be **quick** to listen, slow to speak and slow to become angry.

James 1:19

The Parable of the Sower (around AD 28)

Jesus said, "Listen!" He had something very important to say. He told the story of a farmer who went out to sow some seed. Some seeds fell on the path and birds ate it. Some fell on the rocks and were scorched by the sun. Some fell in thorn bushes and were choked. But some fell on good soil and produced a crop. Jesus explained, "The seed is the word of God" (Luke 8:11). Some people are like seeds on the path. They hear the Word of God, but Satan comes and takes it away. Some are like seeds on the rocks. They receive the Word, but fall away when trials come. Some are like seed sown among thorns. The Word is choked out by worry. But others listen and obey. They receive God's blessings!

You can read this story in Luke, chapter 8!

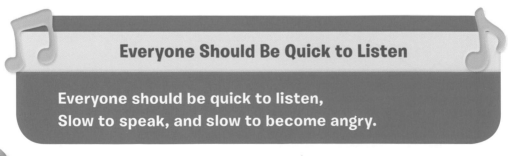

Everyone Should Be Quick to Listen

Everyone should be quick to listen,
Slow to speak, and slow to become angry.

Devotion: Listen to God

Ryan was always talking in class. As Mr. Myers was passing out the tests, Ryan just kept on talking. Mr. Myers said, "Listen carefully. First, read every question, and then begin the test." Everyone did as Mr. Myers said—everyone except for Ryan. He wasn't listening. Within minutes, everyone began to leave the classroom. Ryan wondered how they could possibly be finished! But then, as he got to the last question, he read, "Now go back and only answer question number one."

It's easier to open your ears if your mouth is closed. When you listen, you can learn. But with so many voices calling out in this world, who should you listen to? The voice of God, of course! He speaks through the Bible. So today, be quick to listen and be slow to speak!

🔑 HIDE THE WORD

Everyone should be quick to listen, slow to speak and slow to become angry.
—James 1:19

👁 SEEK THE LORD

Parrot Talk

A parrot listens to what the trainer says, then repeats it back. Maybe we should be more like a parrot. We should learn to be good listeners too. Listening to our teachers helps us grow as Christians. Have your mom read one of the *Hide & Seek* Bible verses to you. Listen carefully! Now, pretend you're a parrot. Repeat the verse back to her word for word. If you miss a word, have her repeat it again. You're learning to be a good listener! If you want to have more fun, have mom give you a cracker if you get the verse right. "Polly want a cracker?"

✝ PRAY TO GOD

Dear Lord, there is so much noise in the world today. With the television booming and radio blaring, it's hard to find a quiet place. But I want to be sure to listen to You. Speak to my heart, Lord, and lead me in the way I should go. Amen.

Show proper **respect** to everyone.

1 Peter 2:17

David and Goliath (around 1025 BC)

Goliath was a very big and powerful man. But he had a lesson to learn about respecting God! Goliath was a Philistine warrior. He stood over nine feet tall! One day, Israel met the Philistine army for battle. Each morning for forty days, Goliath would stand in the valley and shout insults at Israel and their God. He had no respect for them. Goliath was about to find out how powerful God really is! When David heard Goliath mocking God, he marched out to do battle. Although David was just a boy, his God was mighty! David carried a slingshot with him and said, "I come against you in the name of the LORD" (1 Samuel 17:45). Then he hurled a stone at Goliath. *Bam!* David hit him squarely in the head. Down went the giant! Goliath should have respected God's mighty power!

You can read this story in 1 Samuel, chapter 17!

Show Proper Respect

Show proper respect to everyone you meet—
Big or small, short or tall, doesn't matter at all!

Devotion: R-E-S-P-E-C-T

"Lightning can be a very dangerous thing," said Mr. Butler. Mr. Butler was a meteorologist, but we called him the weather man. He had come to visit our school.

"Lightning is a very powerful bolt of electricity," he explained. "It can strike trees and even people. Hundreds of people die each year because they do not use caution during lightning storms. Lightning is very, very powerful and must be respected."

Also, be sure to show proper respect for everyone you meet. All people were created by God and made in His image. For that, they deserve your respect. You should never disrespect others because of the way they look, the language they speak, or the things they have. If we respect others, they will respect us too! Peter said to show R-E-S-P-E-C-T to everyone!

🔑 HIDE THE WORD

Show proper respect to everyone. —1 Peter 2:17

👁 SEEK THE LORD

A Noble Word

The word *lord* can mean "sir" or "master." It is a term used to show respect to a noble person. The word *Lord* is often used in the Bible to show our great respect and love for Jesus. But we can show proper respect to our parents too! Can you think of some ways you can show respect to your mom and dad?

✝ PRAY TO GOD

Dear Lord, I call You *Lord* because I want to show You the great respect You deserve. Lord, there is none like You, nor will there ever be! I call You *Lord* because You alone are great! Amen.

Answers: Obeying; saying "please" and "thank you"

187

Seek first his kingdom and his righteousness, and all these things will be given to you.

Matthew 6:33

Shadrach, Meshach, and Abednego (around 580 BC)

Shadrach, Meshach, and Abednego knew that God trusted them to do what was right. So when the king set up a statue and told all his governors to worship it, Shadrach, Meshach, and Abednego refused. They knew that one day they would answer to God, who was greater than any king. The king ordered them to be thrown into a fiery furnace. They told the king "God . . . is able to save us . . . But even if He does not, . . . we will not serve your gods" (Daniel 3:17–18). Into the fire they went. But they were not burned. They didn't even smell like smoke. God saved them because they obeyed Him!

You can read the whole story in Daniel, chapter 3!

Seek First His Kingdom

Seek first His kingdom and His righteousness.
Seek first His kingdom,
And all these things will be given to you.

Devotion: Do the Right Thing

The Cinema Plaza was fantastic! There were twenty movies playing in different theaters, all at the same time. "Enjoy *Cartoon Town*. I'll be back at 8:30," Cara's mom called as she watched Cara and Allison walk into the theater. As the girls passed a movie poster, Allison said, "Hey, Cara, let's go see the scary movie instead. No one will know." Cara knew her mom trusted her to do the right thing, and she didn't want to let her down. "Nah, *Cartoon Town* is just fine with me," Cara replied, and she stepped up to the ticket booth.

Cara had been trusted to do the right thing. She knew that if she disobeyed her mother, her mother would no longer trust her. She would answer to her mother, not her friend. That's how it is when we're tempted to disobey the Lord. Who will you answer to: the friends who are tempting you, or the Lord? That's right—the Lord! Just remember, seek His righteousness first!

♀ HIDE THE WORD

Seek first his kingdom and his righteousness, and all these things will be given to you.
—Matthew 6:33

👁 SEEK THE LORD

Making Room for God

The Bible says that we must seek first the kingdom of God. It's a matter of putting first things first. Try this exercise. Place a rock in a small plastic bowl. Think it's full? Add some gravel. Is it full now? Let's add some sand. Now it must be full, right? Let's add some water. Now it's full! You have no more room in your bowl.

Now let's do it a different way. Empty the bowl. This time, fill it with water first. Do you have room for the sand, the gravel, or the rock? No! God is like the big rock. If we place Him in our lives first, there is still room for other, less important things. But if we fill our lives with other things *first*, there is no room for God. That's why we must seek Him *first*!

✝ PRAY TO GOD

Dear Lord, You have asked me to seek Your kingdom first. Help me do this. Teach me to walk away from things that crowd You out of my life. And may I always remember that life will be full of good things only if I place You first. Amen.

Whoever can be **trusted** with very little can also be trusted with much.

Luke 16:10

The Parable of the Talents (around AD 30)

A master once trusted his servants with his money. To one, he gave five thousand dollars. To another, he gave two thousand, and to another, he gave one thousand. Then the master went on a long journey. When he returned, he called the three servants in for a report. The one with five thousand had gained five thousand more. The one with two thousand had gained two thousand more. "Well done," said the master. "You have been faithful with a few things; I will put you in charge of many things!" But the man with one thousand dollars had gained nothing. He could not be trusted again!

You can read this story in Matthew, chapter 25!

Can You Be Trusted?

Whoever can be trusted with very little–I know it's true!– Can also be trusted with much. Can you?

Devotion: Trust Is Something You Earn

"Mr. President, what was your very first public office?" asked the fifth grader. The president was visiting a middle school in Nashville, Tennessee. "Now, that's a very good question," responded the president. "My very first public office was held at Dunbar Elementary School, where I was elected treasurer of Mrs. Casto's sixth-grade class. The other students trusted me to collect and turn in the lunch money each day."

To get a big job with big responsibility, you must first show that you can be trusted to do little jobs. The president didn't start by managing a whole country. He started with a small job in the sixth grade. Trust is something you earn every day. If you are faithful to complete the little jobs around the house, then you show everyone you are ready for bigger and more important jobs. Doing a little job well can lead to *big* things!

🔑 HIDE THE WORD

Whoever can be trusted with very little can also be trusted with much. —Luke 16:10

◉ SEEK THE LORD

Seed Sower

God loves trustworthy kids. He loves it when we do what we say we'll do. Let's test our trustworthiness. Find a small plastic cup and place some potting soil in it. Now, plant a seed. (Hint: A few beans from your mom's pantry will work!) Can you be trusted to water it every day? Remember, whoever can be trusted with very little (a seed) can also be trusted with much (a garden). Water the seed each day until it begins to grow. Be a trustworthy kid!

✝ PRAY TO GOD

Dear Lord, I want to do big things for Your kingdom. Help me to be faithful with the little things You give me to do. Only then will I be ready for a big job in Your kingdom. Amen.

u

Do not let any **unwholesome** talk come out of your mouths, but only what is helpful for building others up.

Ephesians 4:29

Job Faces Many Trials (around 2000 BC)

Job faced many trials, yet no unwholesome talk came out of his mouth. Satan was allowed to take his ten children. But Job didn't sin in what he said. Satan was allowed to take all of Job's possessions. But Job didn't sin in what he said. Satan was allowed to make Job sick. Even when Job's wife told him to curse God and die, he didn't sin. In all of his troubles, Job did not speak unkind words to God.

You can read the whole story in the book of Job!

Do Not Let Any Unwholesome Talk Come out of Your Mouths

Do not, do-do-do not,
Do-do-do not let any, let any,
Unwholesome talk
Come out of your ma-ma-ma-mouth!

Devotion: Speak Good Words

The football stadium was packed. Spirits were high, and the team had played their hearts out. The score was tied, 31 to 31, with three seconds left on the clock. The ball was snapped. The kick went up. "No good!" shouted the referee. In the stands behind them, Marcus and his dad heard a young man yelling a lot of really bad words! Dad turned to the young man and said, "Your bad words won't affect the score, but they do affect others around you!"

Your tongue is like a rudder on a ship—small, but with a big purpose—and it must be controlled. It must not speak words that are unwholesome, which are words may that hinder others from seeing Jesus. Always speak good words that encourage others, no matter what happens. Speaking bad words won't change anything. But a good word, spoken at just the right time, can change everything!

HIDE THE WORD

Do not let any unwholesome talk come out of your mouths, but only what is helpful for building others up.
—Ephesians 4:29

👁 SEEK THE LORD

Growing in the Lord

Wholesome words spoken at just the right time make a person "whole." They can build a person up and bring them joy. Jesus always used wholesome talk.

Unwholesome words do just the opposite. They always tear a person down. They can hurt feelings.

Can you think of three wholesome things to say to a friend? (Hint: A compliment that builds up!) Using wholesome talk is a sign you are growing in the Lord.

✝ PRAY TO GOD

Dear Lord, words have such power. When I use kind, wholesome talk and speak in gentle tones, I can build someone up. Help me to never let any unwholesome talk come out of my mouth. Amen.

I am the **vine**; you are the branches . . . apart from me you can do nothing.

John 15:5

Samson, the Strongest Man (around 1050 BC)

Samson's source of power was the Lord. Before Samson was born, an angel came to Samson's mother. The angel told her that her baby would be blessed with the gift of strength in order to do God's work. The angel explained that Samson's hair was never to be cut. She followed the angel's instructions, and Samson soon grew to be the strongest man in the world. He defeated over a thousand men using the jawbone of a donkey! Later, Samson fell in love with a woman named Delilah. Delilah didn't believe in God. When Samson told her the secret of his strength, she told his secret to the enemy, and the enemy cut off his hair. He was powerless!

You can read the whole story in Judges, chapters 13–16!

I Am the Vine

I, I, I, I am the vine. You, you, you, you are the branches.
But I, I, I, I am the vine. Apart from me, you can do nothing.

Devotion: Stay Attached to Jesus

Outside, the storm was growing worse. John heard the rain pouring harder and harder, and the thunder was getting louder and louder. Suddenly, a bolt of lightning lit up the entire night sky. *Boom!* went the thunder; then the lights went out. "Turn on the lights!" cried Bobby, John's little four-year-old brother. "We didn't turn the lights off, Bobby," Mom explained in a comforting voice. "When the electric power is off, the lights won't work."

Your source of strength is the Lord. He is like a vine that feeds all the branches. The branches then feed the grapes. If the grape is cut off from the vine, it dies. Likewise, if you cut yourself off from the Lord, you lose your source of strength. You can do nothing. You are powerless like Samson. But, if you stay attached to Jesus, you're like a lamp that has the electricity on . . . you shine! You can do all things through Christ who strengthens you.

⚷ HIDE THE WORD

I am the vine; you are the branches . . . apart from me you can do nothing. —John 15:5

👁 SEEK THE LORD

Shine On!

David once wrote in Psalm 28:7, "The LORD is my strength." What did he mean? Take a flashlight and turn it on. See how brightly it shines! Now, without turning it off, unscrew the end and remove the batteries. What happens? Without the power supplied by the batteries, the flashlight stops shining. In the very same way, without the power and strength God supplies to us each day, we no longer shine—just like a flashlight without batteries. So let the Lord be your strength and shine, shine, shine!

✝ PRAY TO GOD

Dear Lord, may I never forget that You are my strength from day to day. If I am to grow up and be light in this world, You will have to be my battery! You will supply the strength I will need to shine for You. You are the vine—and the batteries—that supply my strength. Amen.

Worship the Lord your God and serve him only.

Luke 4:8

Elijah and the Prophets of Baal (around 850 BC)

Wicked King Ahab ruled in Israel. He and his evil wife Jezebel worshiped Baal, a false god. Elijah, a prophet of God, told King Ahab that because of his wickedness, it would not rain until Elijah said it would. Elijah challenged the prophets of Baal to meet him on Mt. Carmel. Elijah instructed them to get two bulls to lay on an altar. He told them, "You call on the name of your god, and I will call on the name of the LORD. The god who answers by fire—he is [the one true] God" (1 Kings 18:24). The prophets of Baal called on their god. Nothing happened. They called again and again. Nothing happened. But when Elijah called on the true God, fire fell from heaven, and then the rains began to fall! Everyone then knew who the true God really was.

You can read the whole story in 1 Kings, chapter 18!

O Worship the Lord Your God

O worship the Lord your God
And serve him only.

Devotion: The One True God

"How can it be true?" asked the lieutenant. "Are you 100 percent positive?" Yes, it was true. Marcus Johnson was a double agent. For years, he had been working as a spy for the United States. Now he was working for the enemy. He was selling secrets to other countries! Marcus was arrested, tried in court, and found guilty of treason. You cannot serve two countries. Marcus had betrayed his country.

The Bible is clear: worship the Lord and serve Him only. You cannot serve two masters. That's like being a double agent. You will always favor one or the other. You must serve God and Him alone. The "gods" of this world offer things that begin with a little "g," like gold and things that glitter. But the true God offers you things that begin with a big "G," like Grace and Goodness! Serve the "big G" God!

🔑 HIDE THE WORD

Worship the Lord your God and serve him only.
—Luke 4:8

👁 SEEK THE LORD

Favorite Things

Who is first on your list of favorite people? It's easy to find out. Let's make a list. Don't read any further until you have made a list of your top ten favorite people. Finished? Now, make a list of your ten most favorite things to do. Don't read any further until you have done this. Finished? Is Jesus one of your favorite people? Is sharing the love of Jesus one of your favorite things to do? Make sure Jesus is at the top your list and serve Him only!

✝ PRAY TO GOD

Dear Lord, so many times I get distracted by the things of this world. Help me worship you and serve you only. Teach me to do the things you ask all Christians to do: to love you first, to seek you first, and to serve you always! Amen.

If anything is eXcellent or praiseworthy—think about such things.

Philippians 4:8

Moses Receives the Ten Commandments (around 1445 BC)

God listed His standards for excellence in the Ten Commandments. When Moses received the Ten Commandments from God, the Lord said, "I am the LORD your God, who brought you out of Egypt" (Exodus 20:2). These Ten Commandments were, and still are, God's standard of excellent behavior for every boy and girl. They teach His people how to treat each other and how to honor God. They also help us see why we need a Savior. God sets the standard very high!

You can read this story in Exodus, chapter 20!

If Anything Is Excellent

If anything is excellent,
If anything is praiseworthy,
If anything is excellent or praiseworthy,
Think about such things!

Devotion: Seek Good in God's Eyes

Mrs. Johnson had an excellent class with twenty of the most well-mannered kids you'd ever find. She set the standard very high. She expected excellence in all of their subjects, and she expected excellence in their behavior. When the students met her standard, they were excellent!

A steering wheel controls a car. But what controls the mind? What you put into it! If something is excellent in God's eyes, you should think about it. If something is worthy of praise, you should think about it. But there are Web sites, television shows, movies, and magazines that are not excellent or praiseworthy in God's sight. Don't give them a second thought! Seek God's kind of excellence!

⚷ HIDE THE WORD

If anything is excellent or praiseworthy—think about such things. —Philippians 4:8

👁 SEEK THE LORD

Spiritual Thinking Cap

Let's put on our spiritual thinking cap and think about things that are excellent to God. How about faith? Is it excellent to have faith in God like David did? Of course it is! How about love? Is it excellent to love your neighbor like the Good Samaritan did? Right again! Can you think of some more things that are excellent to God? (Hint: Courage, patience, self-control, . . .)

✝ PRAY TO GOD

Dear Lord, as I go through each day, I think about so many things. I think about what I'll eat, and who I'll meet. Help me to think about the things that are excellent in Your sight. May I think about Jesus, the One who is excellent and worthy of my praise! Amen.

Don't let anyone look down on you because you are **young**, but set an example for the believers in speech, in life, in love, in faith and in purity.

1 Timothy 4:12

Paul, a Good Example (around AD 55)

Paul wrote a letter to the church at Corinth. In it, he makes a remarkable statement. It is one that few of us would dare make. He said, "Follow my example, as I follow the example of Christ" (1 Corinthians 11:1). Paul was learning and obeying the teachings of Jesus and living them out in his daily life. His speech, love, and faith showed the world he was a Christian!

You can read the letter Paul wrote in 1 Corinthians!

Don't Let Anyone Look Down on You

Don't let anyone look down on you
Because, because, because you are young.
No! Don't let anyone look down on you.

Devotion: Set a Good Example

Celebrities can have a great influence on many people. They set examples that many will follow. If they are polite and you see that example, perhaps you will be polite. If they wear their hair a certain way or dress a certain way, a lot of people will follow. You, too, can influence the people around you with your actions. And others can learn from your example.

Is your life a good example of the Christian life? As a believer, you need to set a good example. Your speech needs to be clean and pure. Your life needs to be free from sinful habits. And your faith should be growing. Even though you are young, you can set a good example for others. You're never too young to be a good example!

? HIDE THE WORD

Don't let anyone look down on you because you are young, but set an example for the believers in speech, in life, in love, in faith and in purity.
—1 Timothy 4:12

◉ SEEK THE LORD

Be a Good Example

How old are you? Did you know that you're never too young to set a good example for others? They may not know what it means to be a Christian, but when you are kind, people will want to be around you. When you use wholesome words, they will want to be like you. You may be the only Christian they will know, so be a good example. You never know who's watching.

In what ways can you be a good example at home? How about at school or church? How about at bedtime?

✝ PRAY TO GOD

Dear Lord, I want to be a good example for others. May my speech be wholesome and my life full of good deeds. May I demonstrate my faith in You every day. Please give me the heart to love others in a way that is pleasing to You. Amen.

Answers: Obey; listen; pray.

Zacchaeus, come down immediately.

Luke 19:5

Zacchaeus Sees Jesus (around AD 30)

Once, Jesus passed through Jericho on His way to Jerusalem. Jericho was the home of Zacchaeus, a tax collector. Zacchaeus wanted to see Jesus, but he was very short. He could not see over the crowds, so he climbed up in a sycamore tree. From there, he could see. When Jesus passed by, He saw Zacchaeus and said, "Come down immediately. I must stay at your house today" (Luke 19:5). Zacchaeus welcomed Jesus and was saved.

You can read this story in Luke, chapter 19!

Zacchaeus Was a Wee Little Man

Zacchaeus was a wee little man.
A wee little man was he.
He climbed up in a sycamore tree,
For the Lord he wanted to see.
And as the Lord passed by his way,
He looked up in the tree,
And Jesus said, "Zacchaeus, come down immediately."

Devotion: Don't Let Anything Stand in Your Way

When you're a kid living in an adult world, it can be very frustrating. For instance, you're watching the Christmas parade pass by. Suddenly, there's a really exciting moment. All the adults jump up to watch. You can't see anything! You're not tall enough. Sometimes, you wish you could just take a ladder to the parade. Then you could see!

Do you want to see Jesus? Zacchaeus did! He wasn't going to let anything stand in his way, so don't let anything stand in *your* way. You're not too young; you're not too old. You can't be too short or tall, fat or thin. If you want to see Jesus, you can find Him in the Bible. He's looking for you too!

HIDE THE WORD

Zacchaeus, come down immediately.
—Luke 19:5

👁 SEEK THE LORD

Road Block

Open the door to your room. Walk out of your room and back into it. That was easy! Now shut the door. Access to your room is now blocked. You can't see in or out. Until that door is opened, no one can get in or see in. Sometimes, things can come between you and a wholehearted relationship with Jesus. It's like a closed door. It could be a person at school or an activity. Ask the Lord to help you "open the door" to whatever it is blocking the way. Pray the prayer below out loud.

✝ PRAY TO GOD

Lord, I love You. I want to stand up for You wherever I go. But sometimes my fear becomes a road block. It stands between me and someone who needs to know about Jesus. Lord, give me the courage to tell others about my faith in Jesus. And like Zacchaeus, don't let the crowd keep me from Jesus! Amen.

My Memorization Checklist: Old Testament Verses

A How **Awesome** is the LORD Most High. —Psalm 47:2 ☐ Date: _____

B On my **Bed** I remember you; I think of
you through the watches of the night. —Psalm 63:6 ☐ Date: _____

C God **Created** the heavens and the earth. —Genesis 1:1 ☐ Date: _____

D My mouth will **Declare** your praise. —Psalm 51:15 ☐ Date: _____

E Let **Everything** that has breath
praise the LORD. —Psalm 150:6 ☐ Date: _____

F A **Friend** loves at all times. —Proverbs 17:17 ☐ Date: _____

G A **Gentle** answer turns away wrath. —Proverbs 15:1 ☐ Date: _____

H Love the LORD your God with all
your **Heart** and with all your soul
and with all your strength. —Deuteronomy 6:5 ☐ Date: _____

I So God created man in his own **Image**. —Genesis 1:27 ☐ Date: _____

J The **Joy** of the LORD is your strength. —Nehemiah 8:10 ☐ Date: _____

K **Keep** my commands and you will live. —Proverbs 4:4 ☐ Date: _____

L Your word is a **Lamp** to my feet
and a light for my path. —Psalm 119:105 ☐ Date: _____

M "For **My** thoughts are not your thoughts,
neither are your ways my ways,"
declares the LORD. —Isaiah 55:8 ☐ Date: _____

N The **Name** of the LORD is a strong tower;
the righteous run to it and are safe. —Proverbs 18:10 ☐ Date: _____

O To **Obey** is better than sacrifice. —1 Samuel 15:22 ☐ Date: _____

P "For I know the **Plans** I have for you,"
declares the LORD. —Jeremiah 29:11 ☐ Date: _____

Q He will **Quiet** you with his love. —Zephaniah 3:17 ☐ Date: _____

R **Remember** your Creator in the
days of your youth. —Ecclesiastes 12:1 ☐ Date: _____

S The LORD is my **Shepherd**,
I shall not be in want. —Psalm 23:1 ☐ Date: _____

T Give **Thanks** to the LORD, for he is good. —Psalm 136:1 ☐ Date: _____

U Trust in the LORD with all your heart and
lean not on your own **Understanding**. —Proverbs 3:5 ☐ Date: _____

V In the morning, O LORD,
you hear my **Voice**. —Psalm 5:3 ☐ Date: _____

W As for God, his **Way** is perfect;
the word of the LORD is flawless. —2 Samuel 22:31 ☐ Date: _____

X Glorify the LORD with me;
let us **eXalt** his name together. —Psalm 34:3 ☐ Date: _____

Y **You** are my hiding place;
you will protect me from trouble. —Psalm 32:7 ☐ Date: _____

Z It is not good to have **Zeal**
without knowledge. —Proverbs 19:2 ☐ Date: _____

My Memorization Checklist: New Testament Verses

a And we know that in **all** things God works for the good of those who love him. —Romans 8:28 ☐ Date: _____

b How **beautiful** are the feet of those who bring good news! —Romans 10:15 ☐ Date: _____

c Let the little **children** come to me. —Matthew 19:14 ☐ Date: _____

d **Do** to others what you would have them do to you. —Matthew 7:12 ☐ Date: _____

e **Everyone** who calls on the name of the Lord will be saved. —Romans 10:13 ☐ Date: _____

f **Forgive** as the Lord forgave you. —Colossians 3:13 ☐ Date: _____

g **Give**, and it will be given to you. —Luke 6:38 ☐ Date: _____

h The Lord is my **helper**; I will not be afraid. —Hebrews 13:6 ☐ Date: _____

i What is **impossible** with men is possible with God. —Luke 18:27 ☐ Date: _____

j **Jesus** answered, . . . "You must be born again." —John 3:5–7 ☐ Date: _____

k Always try to be **kind** to each other and to everyone else. —1 Thessalonians 5:15 ☐ Date: _____

l For God so **loved** the world that he gave his one and only Son, that whoever believes in him shall not perish but have eternal life. —John 3:16 ☐ Date: _____

m Be **merciful**, just as your Father is merciful. —Luke 6:36 ☐ Date: _____

n   Love your **neighbor** as yourself. —Matthew 19:19   ☐ Date: _____

o   Children, **obey** your parents in the Lord. —Ephesians 6:1   ☐ Date: _____

p   Be **patient**, bearing with one another in love.
    —Ephesians 4:2   ☐ Date: _____

q   Everyone should be **quick** to listen,
    slow to speak and slow to become angry. —James 1:19   ☐ Date: _____

r   Show proper **respect** to everyone. —1 Peter 2:17   ☐ Date: _____

s   **Seek** first his kingdom and his righteousness,
    and all these things will be given to you.   Matthew 6:33   ☐ Date: _____

t   Whoever can be **trusted** with very little
    can also be trusted with much. —Luke 16:10   ☐ Date: _____

u   Do not let any **unwholesome** talk come
    out of your mouths, but only what is
    helpful for building others up. —Ephesians 4:29   ☐ Date: _____

v   I am the **vine**; you are the branches . . .
    apart from me you can do nothing. —John 15:5   ☐ Date: _____

w   **Worship** the Lord your God
    and serve him only. —Luke 4:8   ☐ Date: _____

x   If anything is **eXcellent** or
    praiseworthy—think about such things. —Philippians 4:8   ☐ Date: _____

y   Don't let anyone look down on you because you are
    young, but set an example for the believers in speech,
    in life, in love, in faith and in purity. —1 Timothy 4:12   ☐ Date: _____

z   **Zacchaeus**, come down immediately. —Luke 19:5   ☐ Date: _____